My name is
AF584374

Track the letter and colour each picture when you have completed the matching page in your work book.

Mm Nn Oo
Pp Qq Rr
Ss Tt Uu
Vv Ww Xx
Yy Zz

l

Trace.

One stroke

Find l.

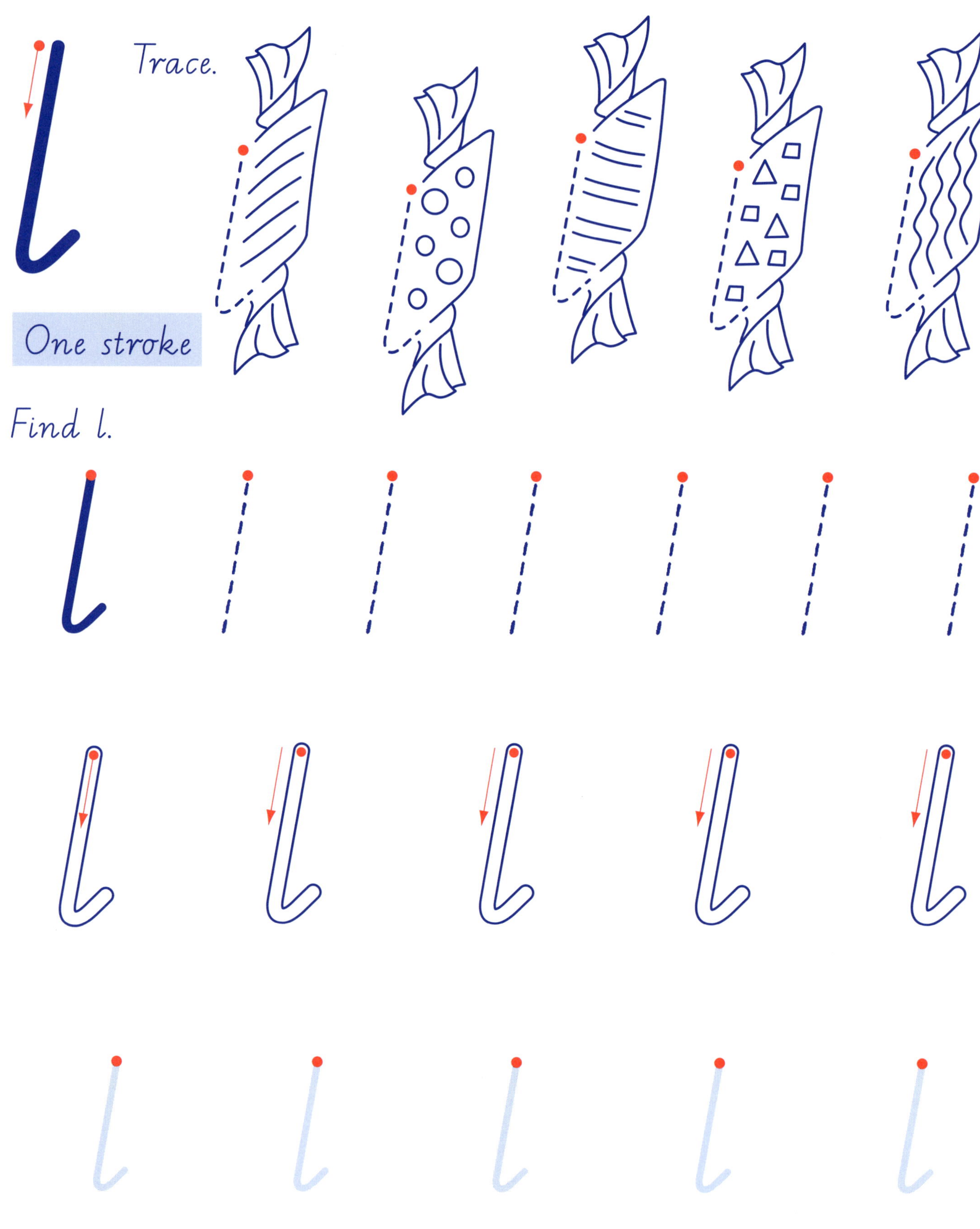

Try your own. Put a ✓ under your best l.

l L
a head and
body letter
lamp
L
Give the fairies their wands.

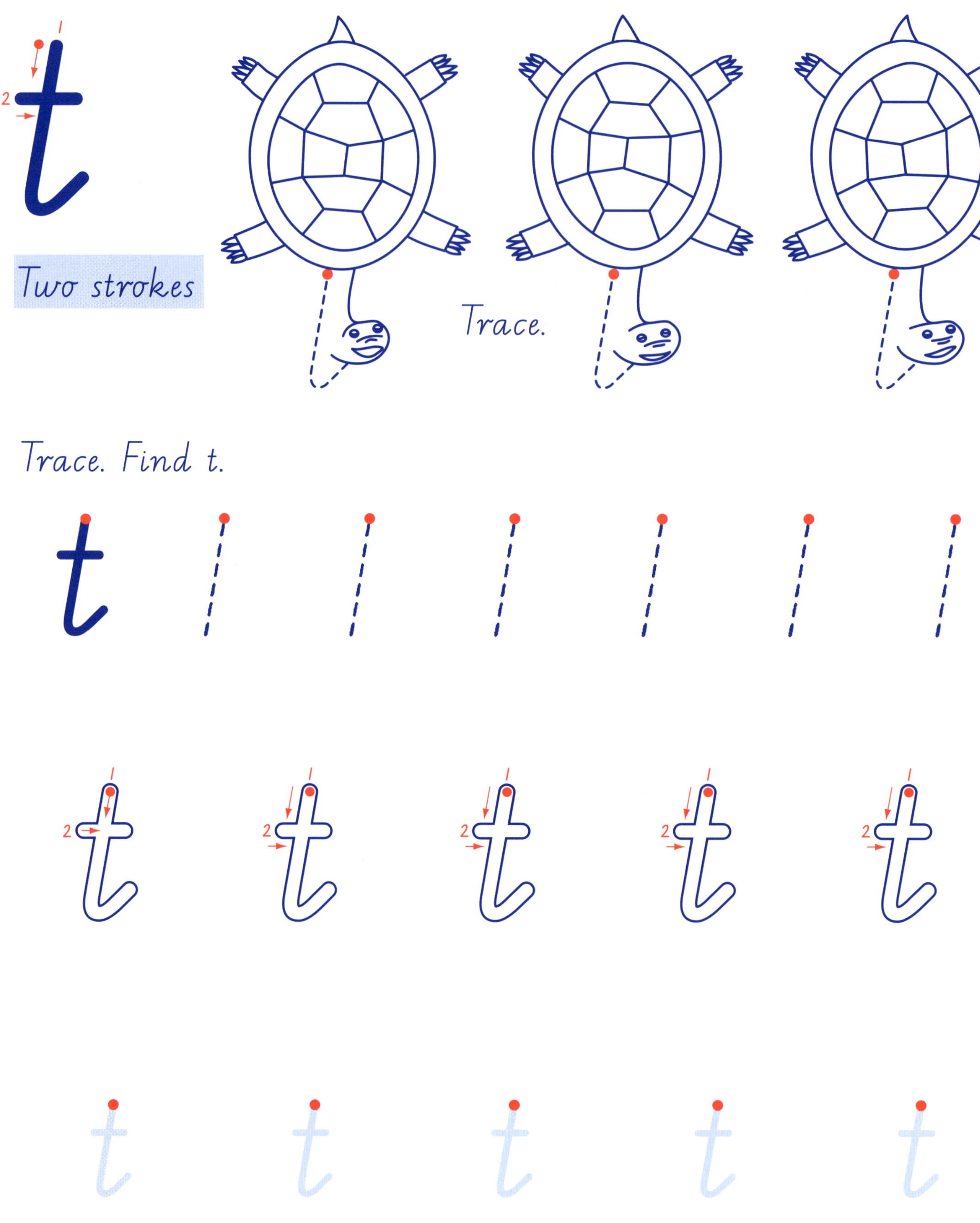

Try your own. Circle your best (t).

t

t T
a head and
body letter
t
tree
T
1
2
t t t t t

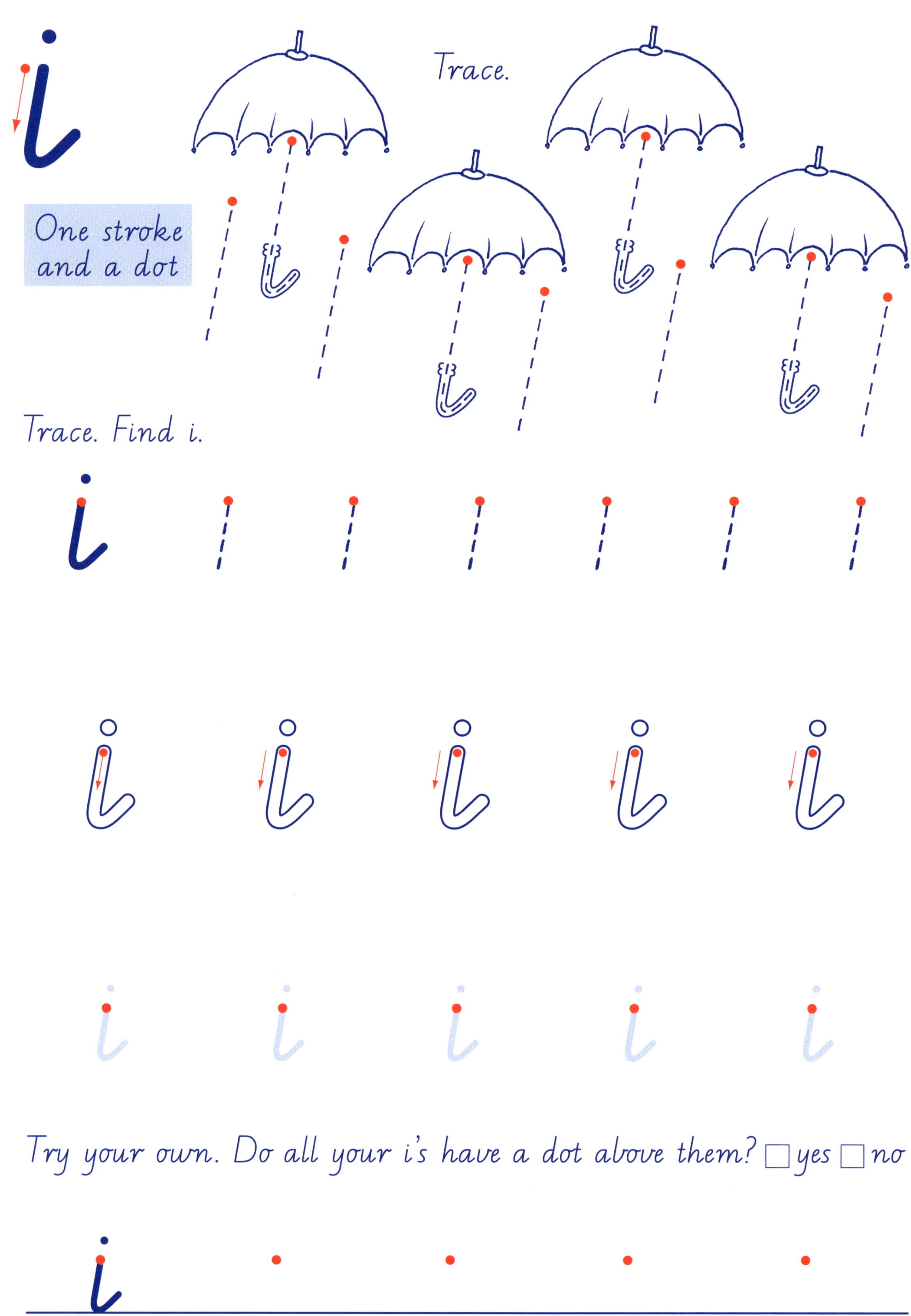
i
One stroke and a dot
Trace.
Trace. Find i.
Try your own. Do all your i's have a dot above them? ☐ yes ☐ no

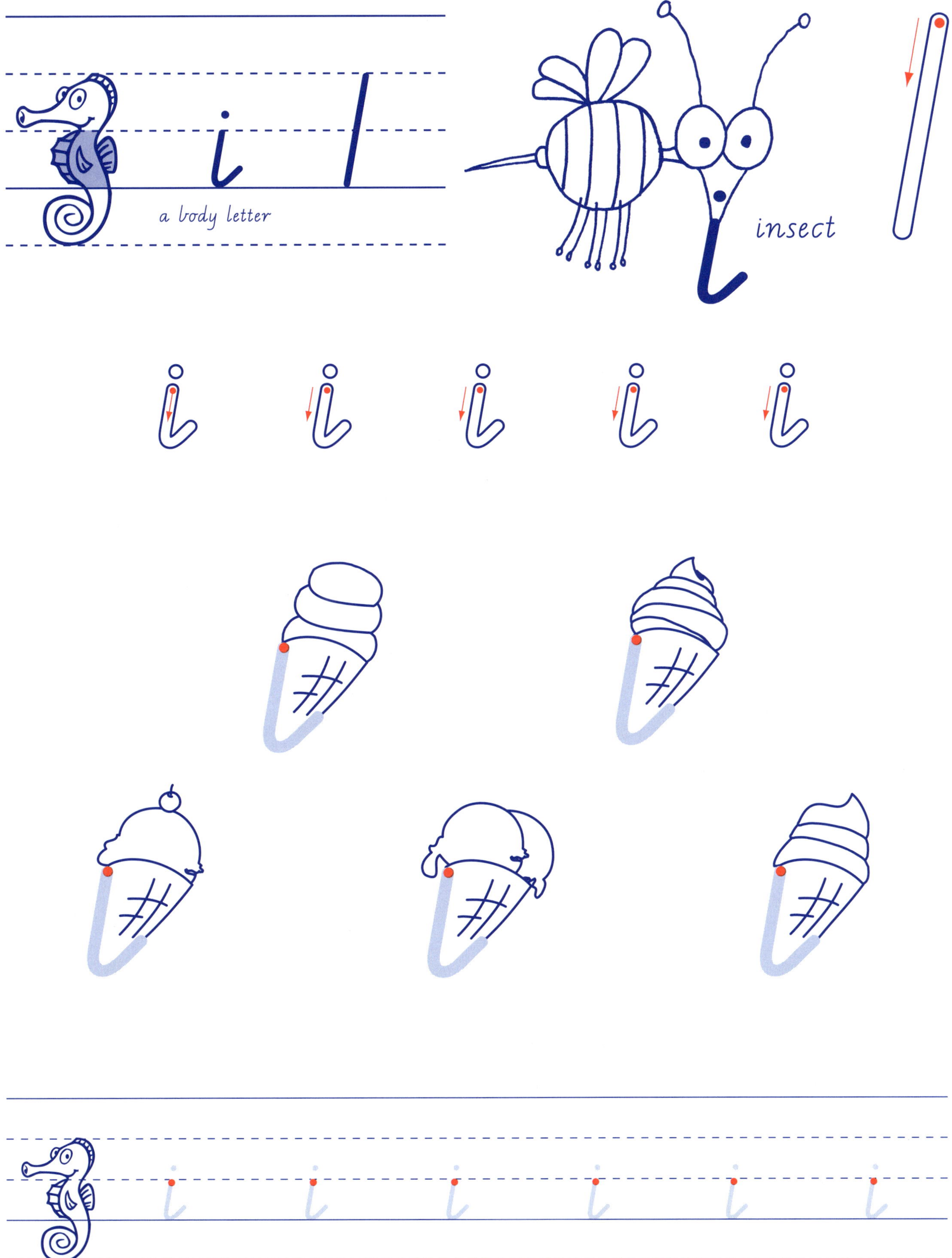
i l
a body letter
insect

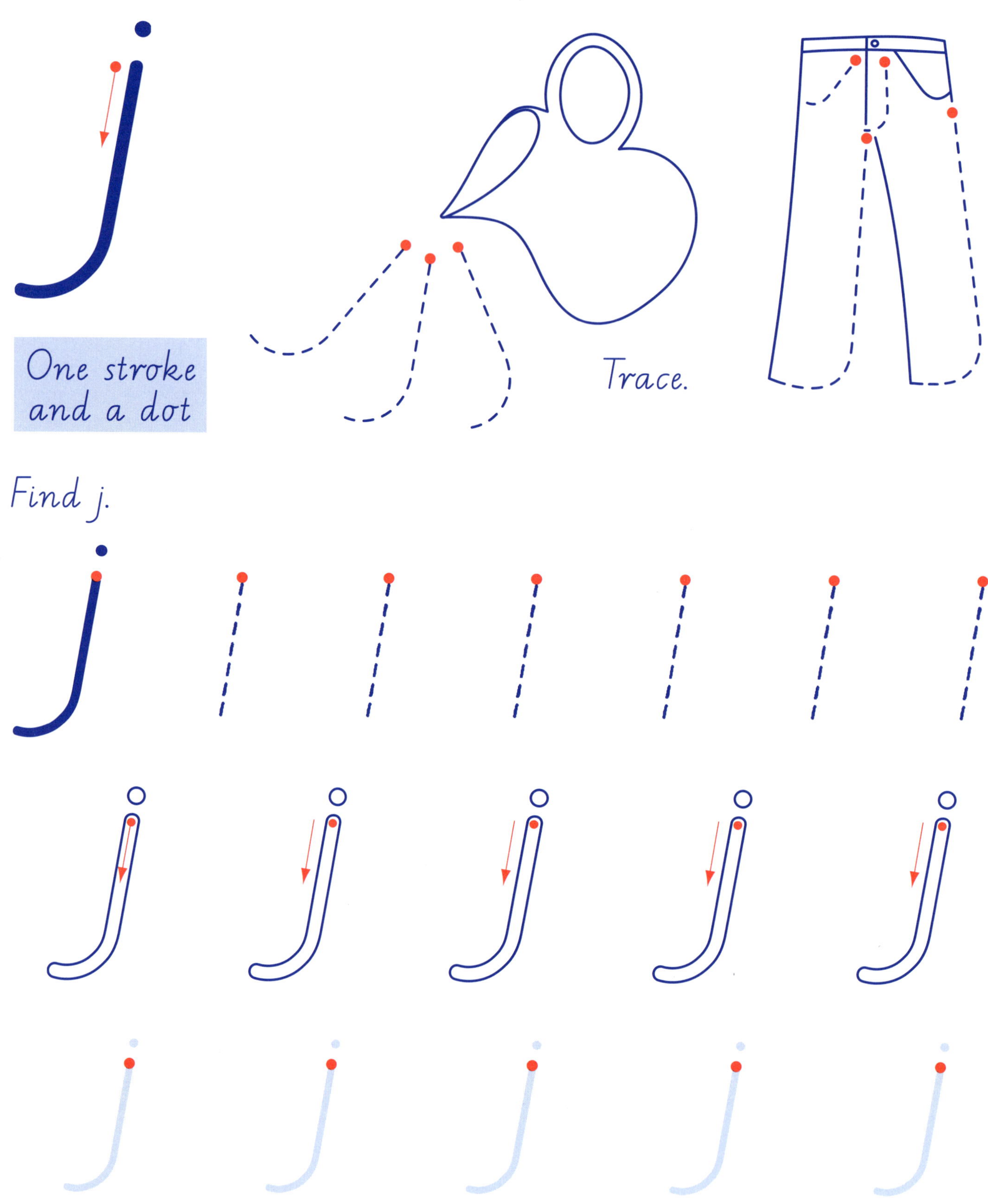

Try your own. ✓ the j that has the smoothest tail.

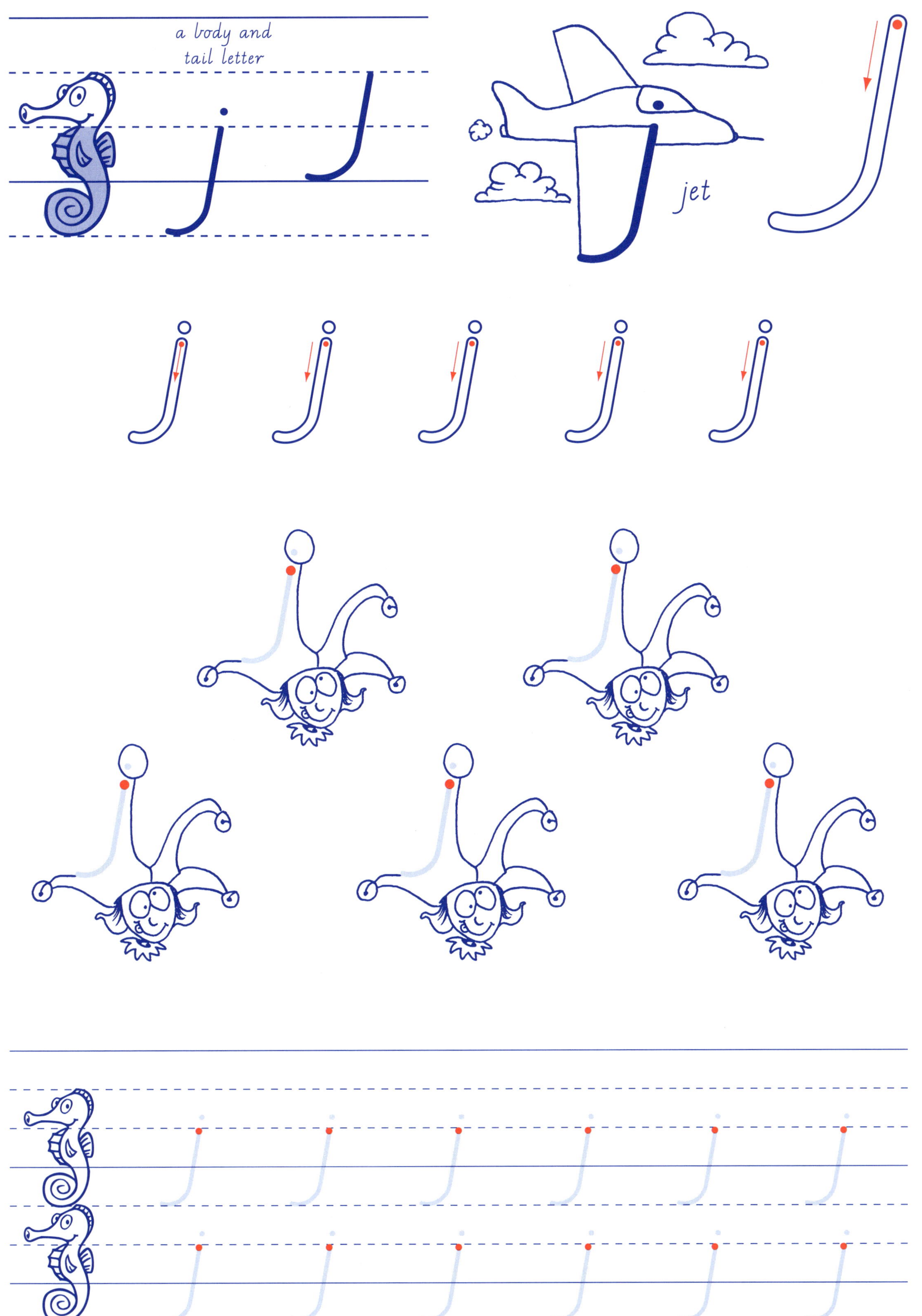
a body and
tail letter
j
jet

m

One stroke

Trace. Colour the wedges of cake.

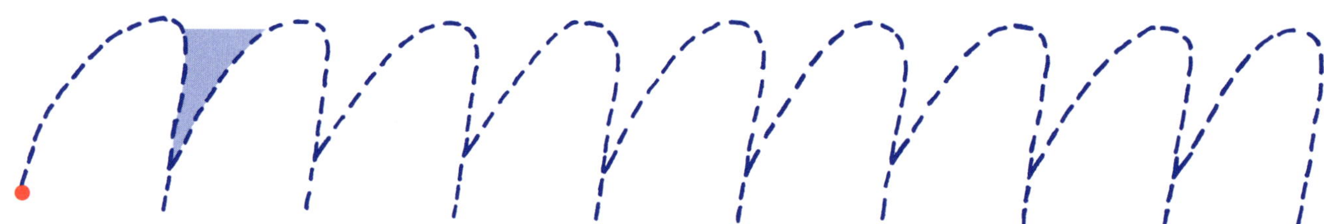

Trace. Find the m's.

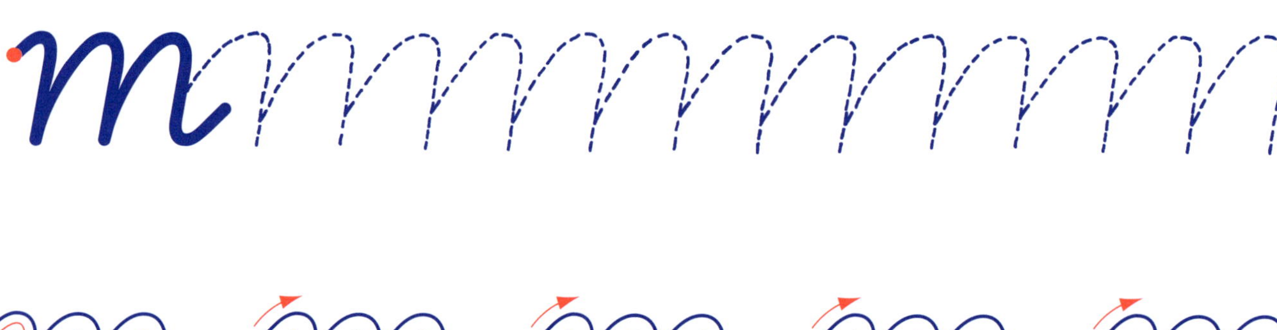

Try your own. Draw a moon under your best m.

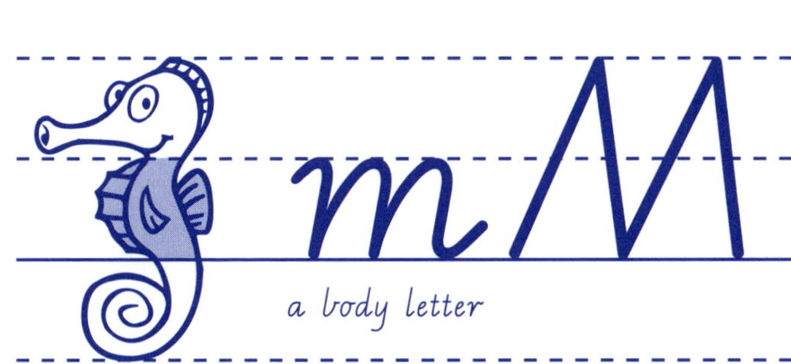

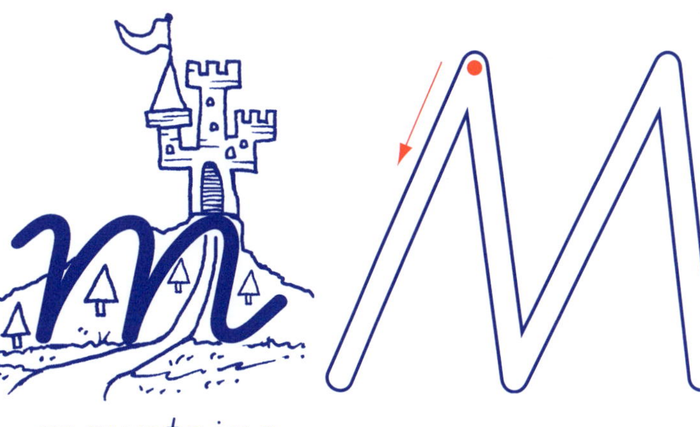

mountains

m m m m m

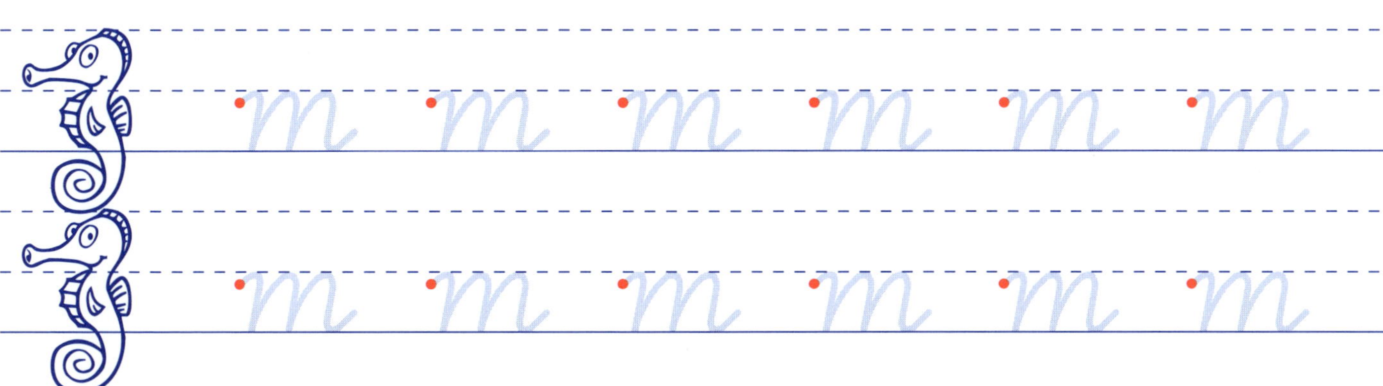

n

One stroke

Track.

Trace the hops using 3 different colours.

Trace. Find the n's.

Try your own. ✓ your best n.

n

n N
a body letter
n
nest
N
n n n n n
n n n n n n
n n n n n n

Trace your finger along the hops.
Then use a crayon to trace the hops.

One stroke

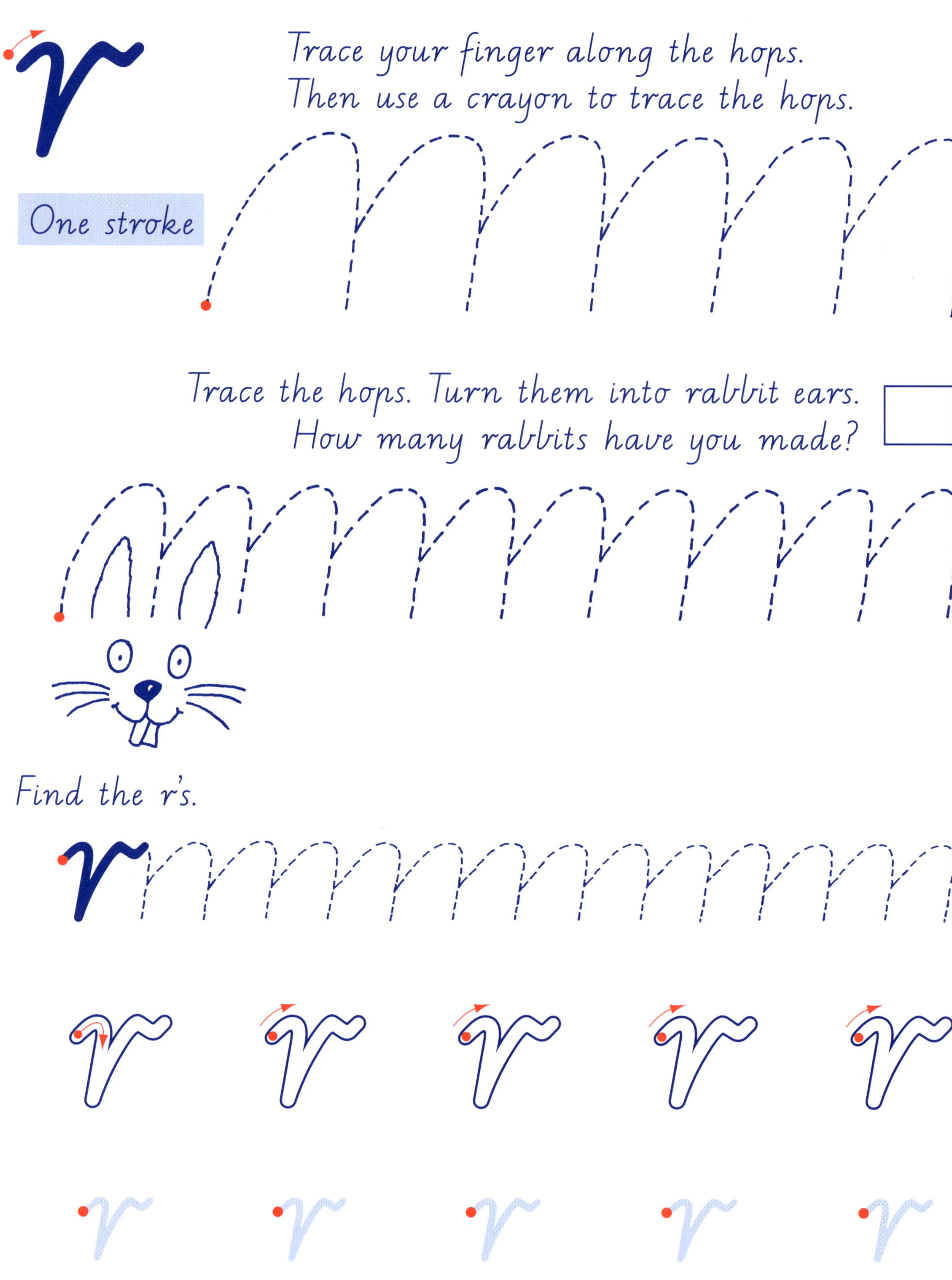

Trace the hops. Turn them into rabbit ears.
How many rabbits have you made?

Find the r's.

Try your own. Draw a red line underneath your best r.

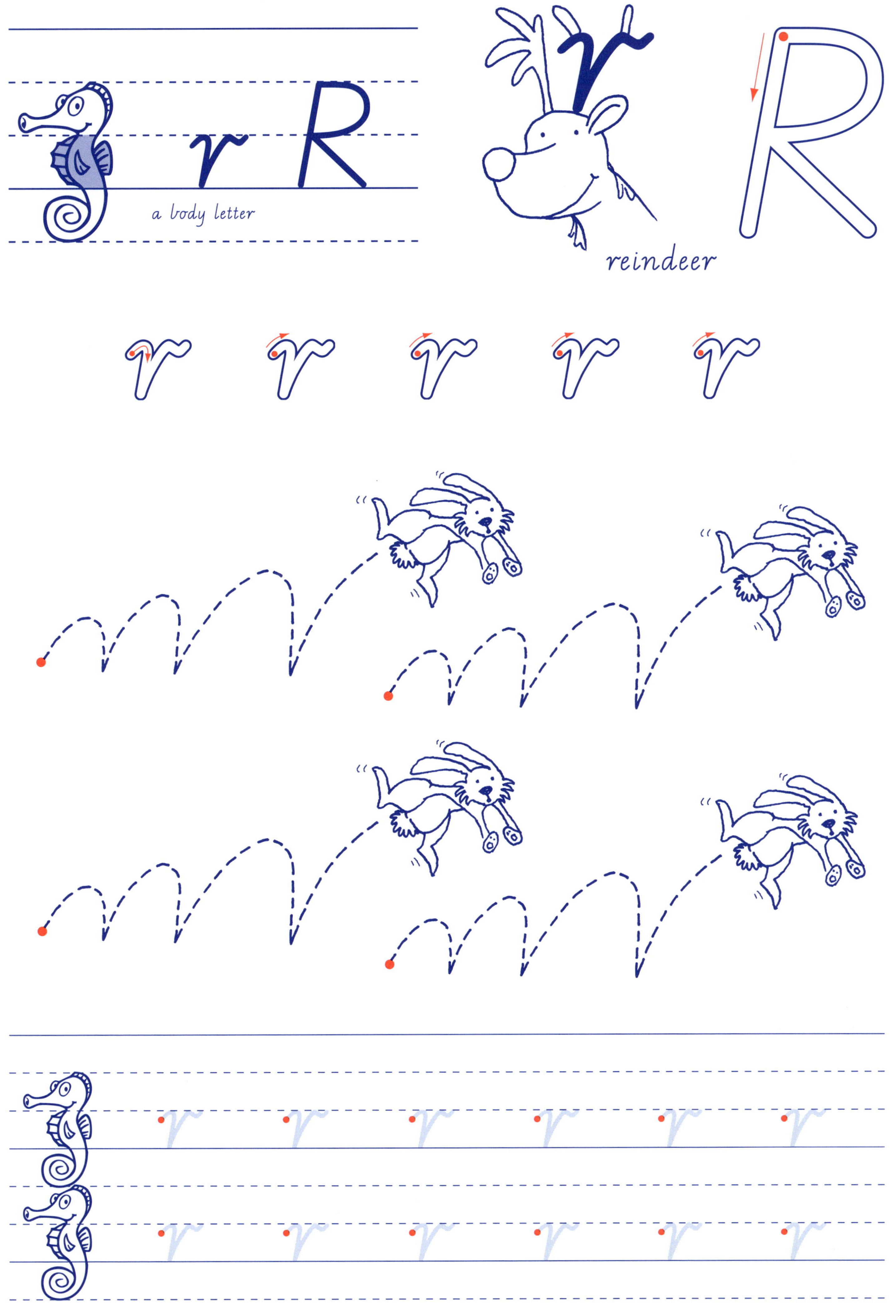

r R
a body letter
reindeer

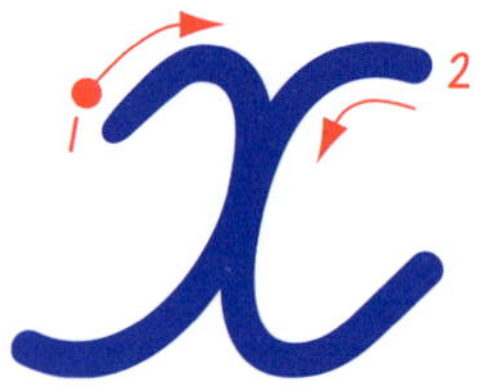

x

Two strokes

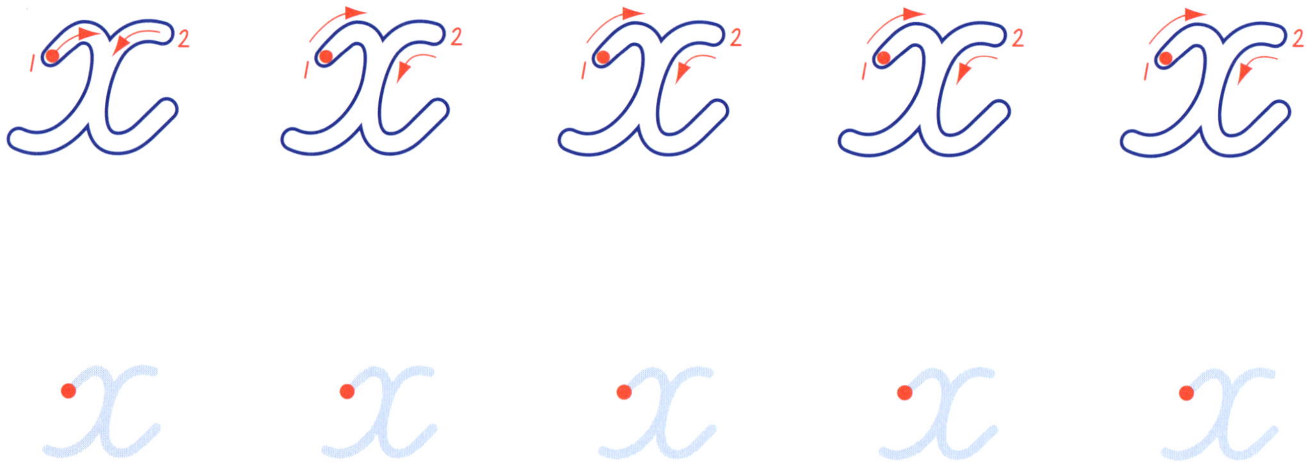

Try your own. Put a box around your best x.

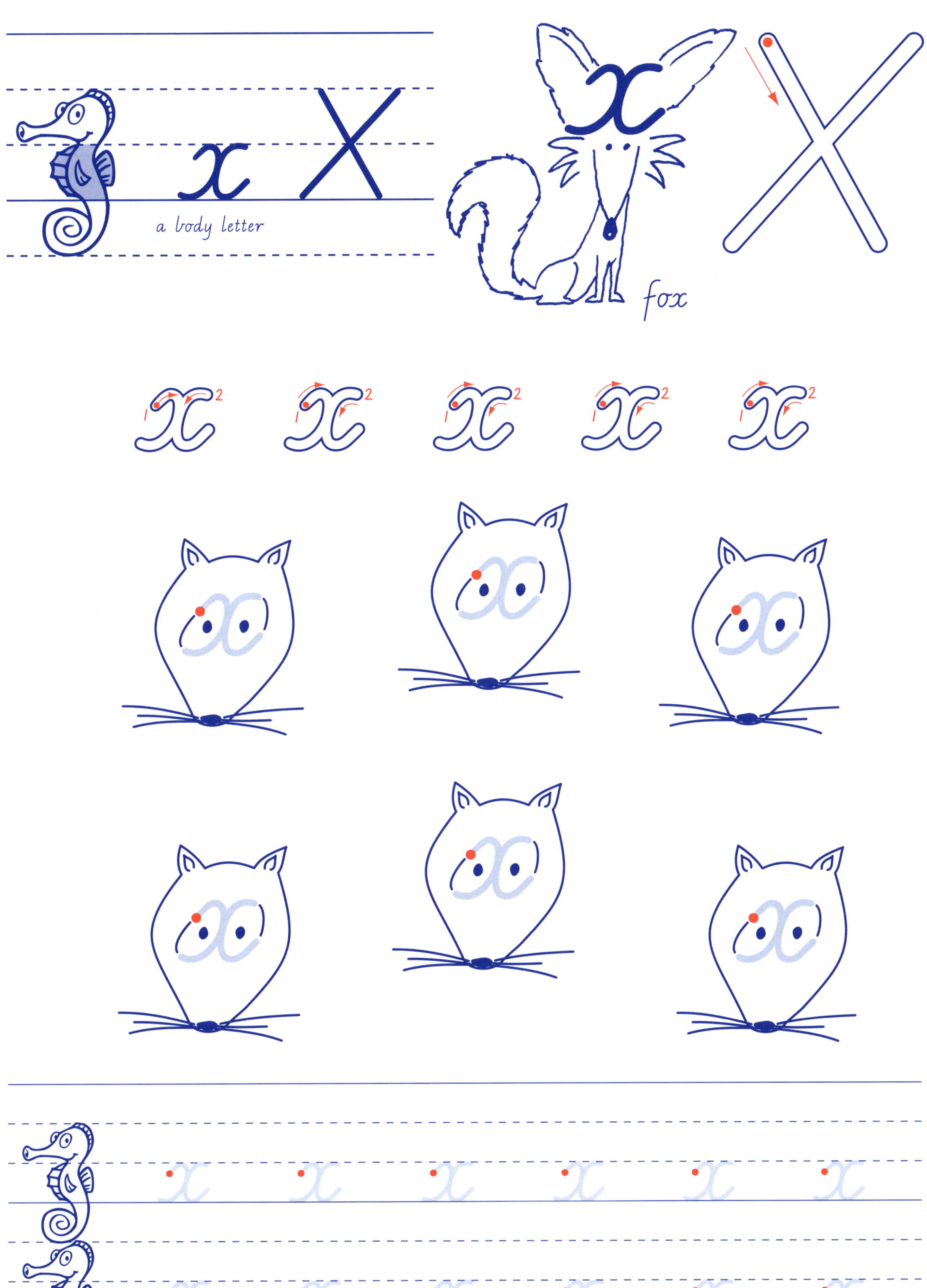
x X
a body letter
fox
1 2

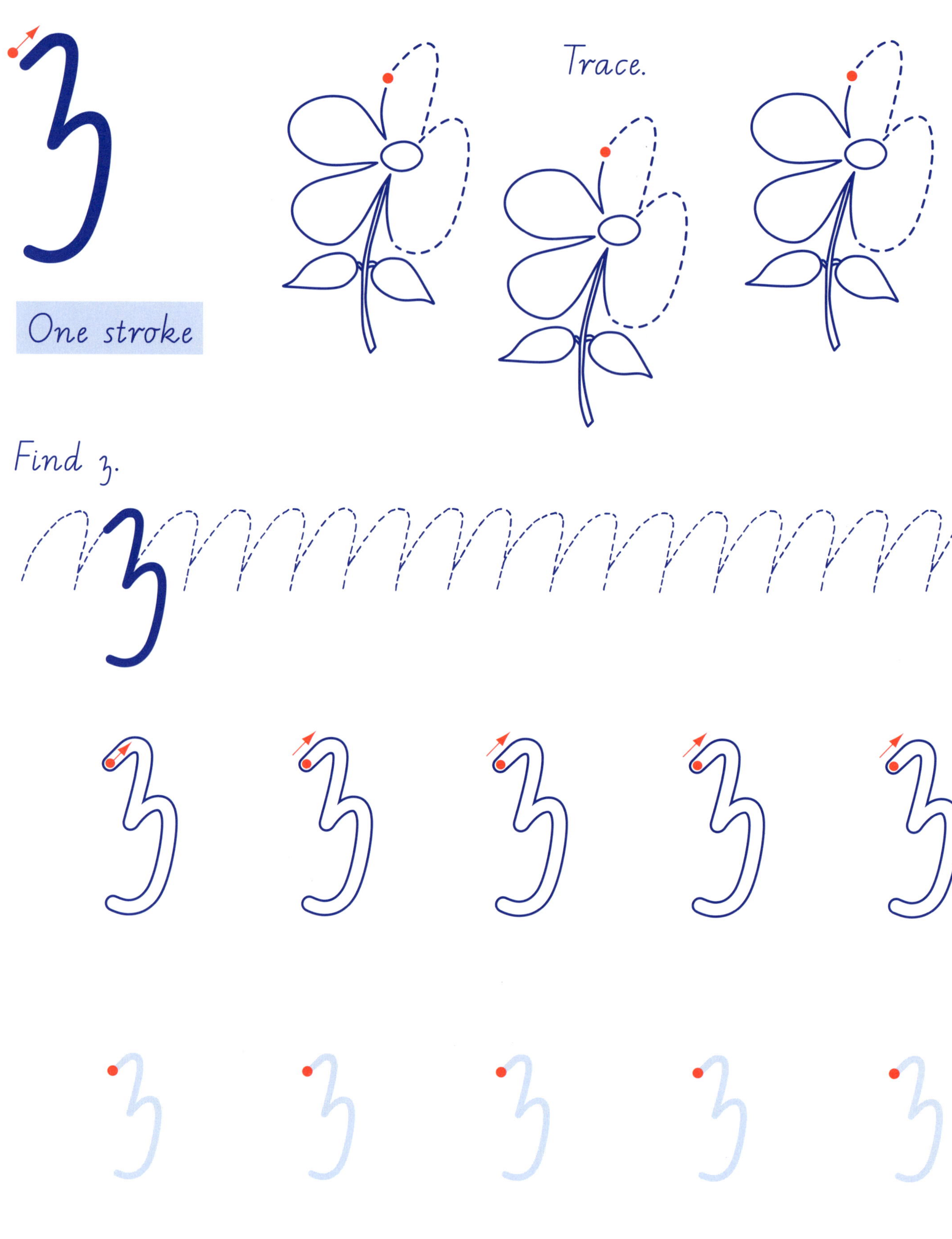

Try your own. Draw a ✳ above your best z.

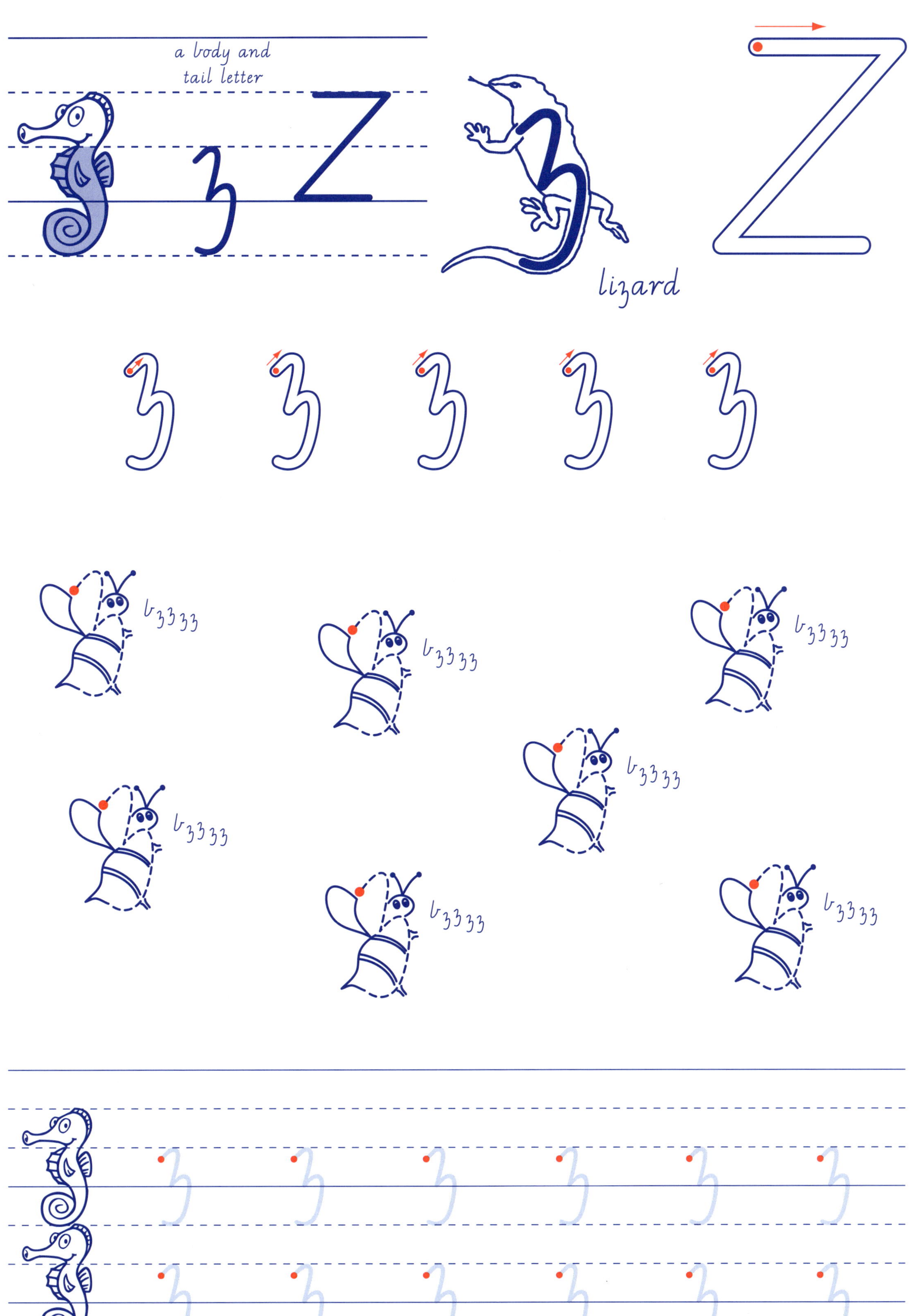
a body and
tail letter
z Z
lizard
bzzzz
bzzzz
bzzzz
bzzzz
bzzzz
bzzzz
bzzzz

h

One stroke

Try your own. Draw a ♡ inside your best h.

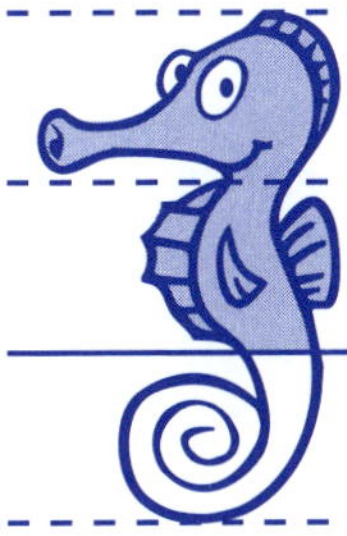

h H

a head and
body letter

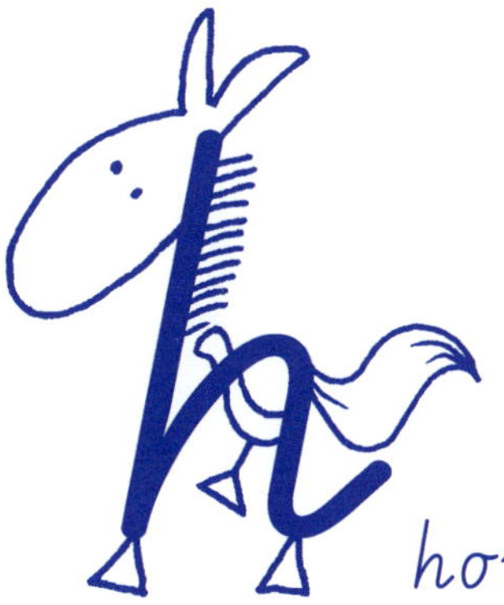

horse

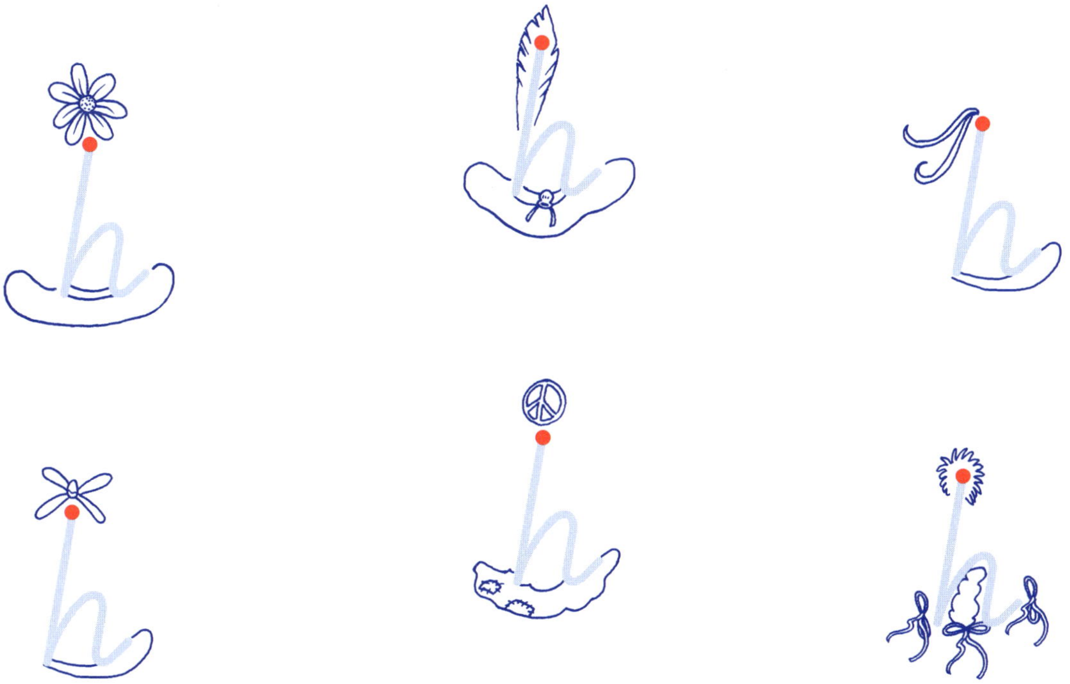

H

h h h h h

h h h h h h

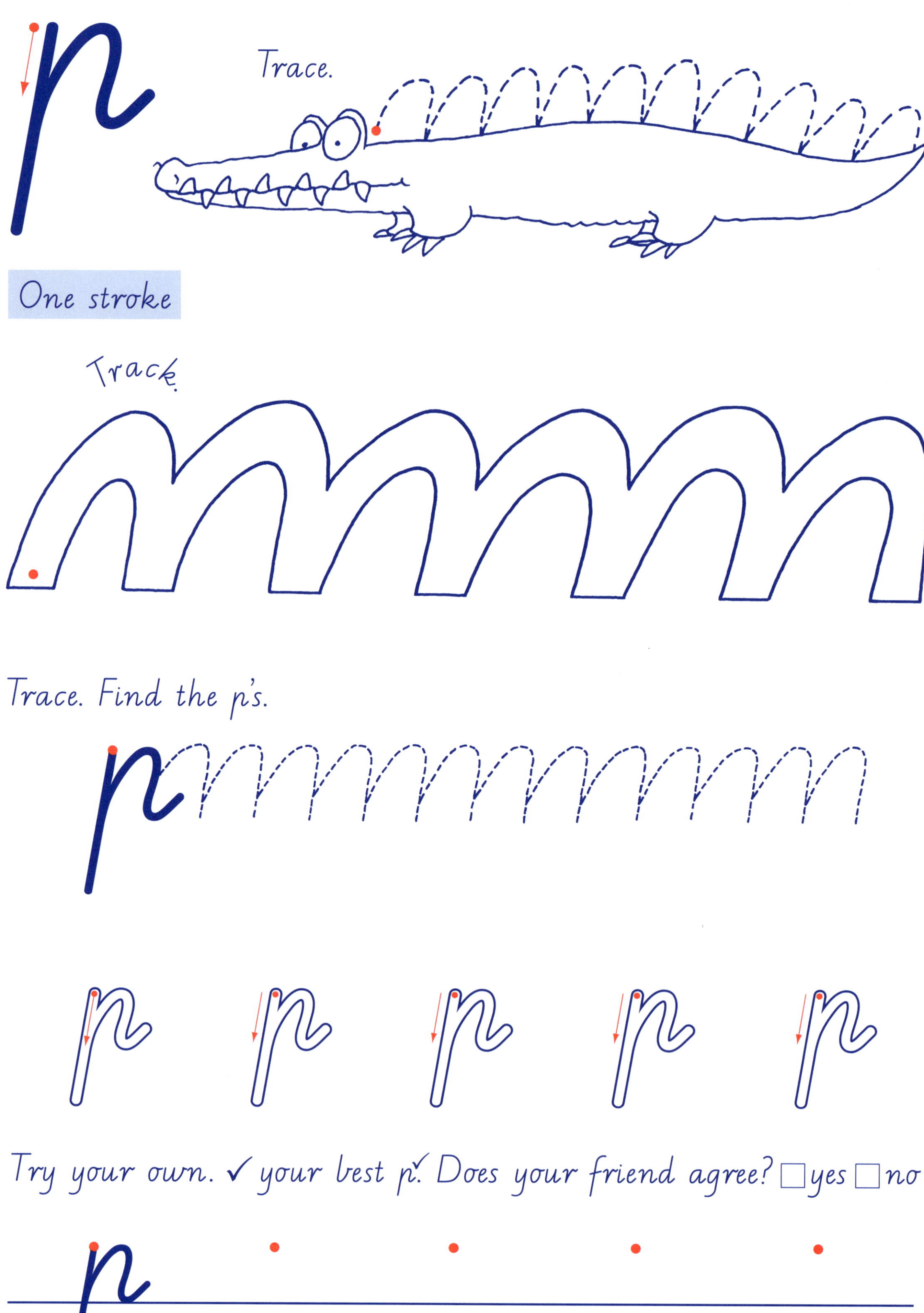
p
Trace.
One stroke
Track.
Trace. Find the p's.
Try your own. ✓ your best p. Does your friend agree? ☐ yes ☐ no

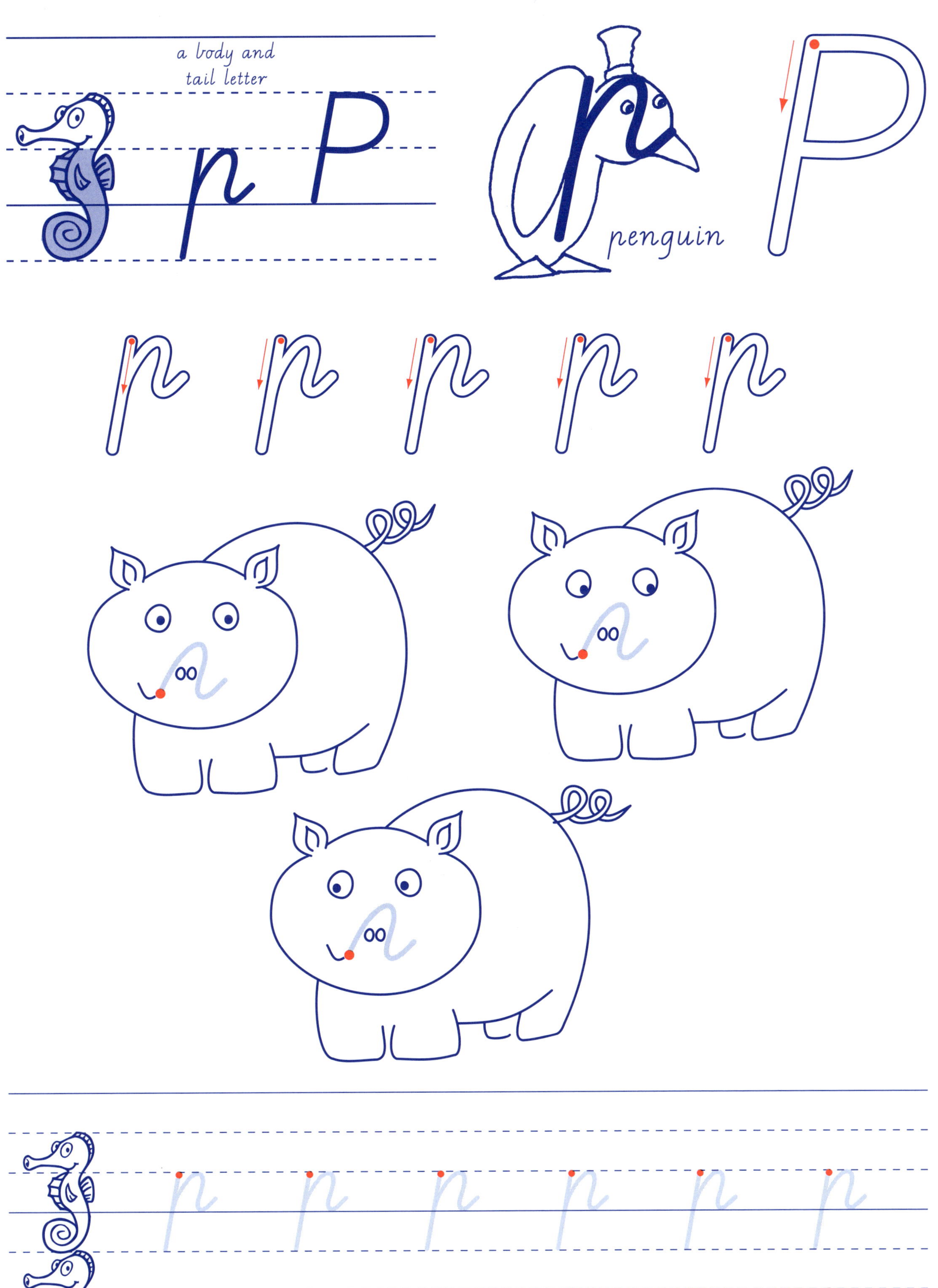
a body and
tail letter
p P
penguin

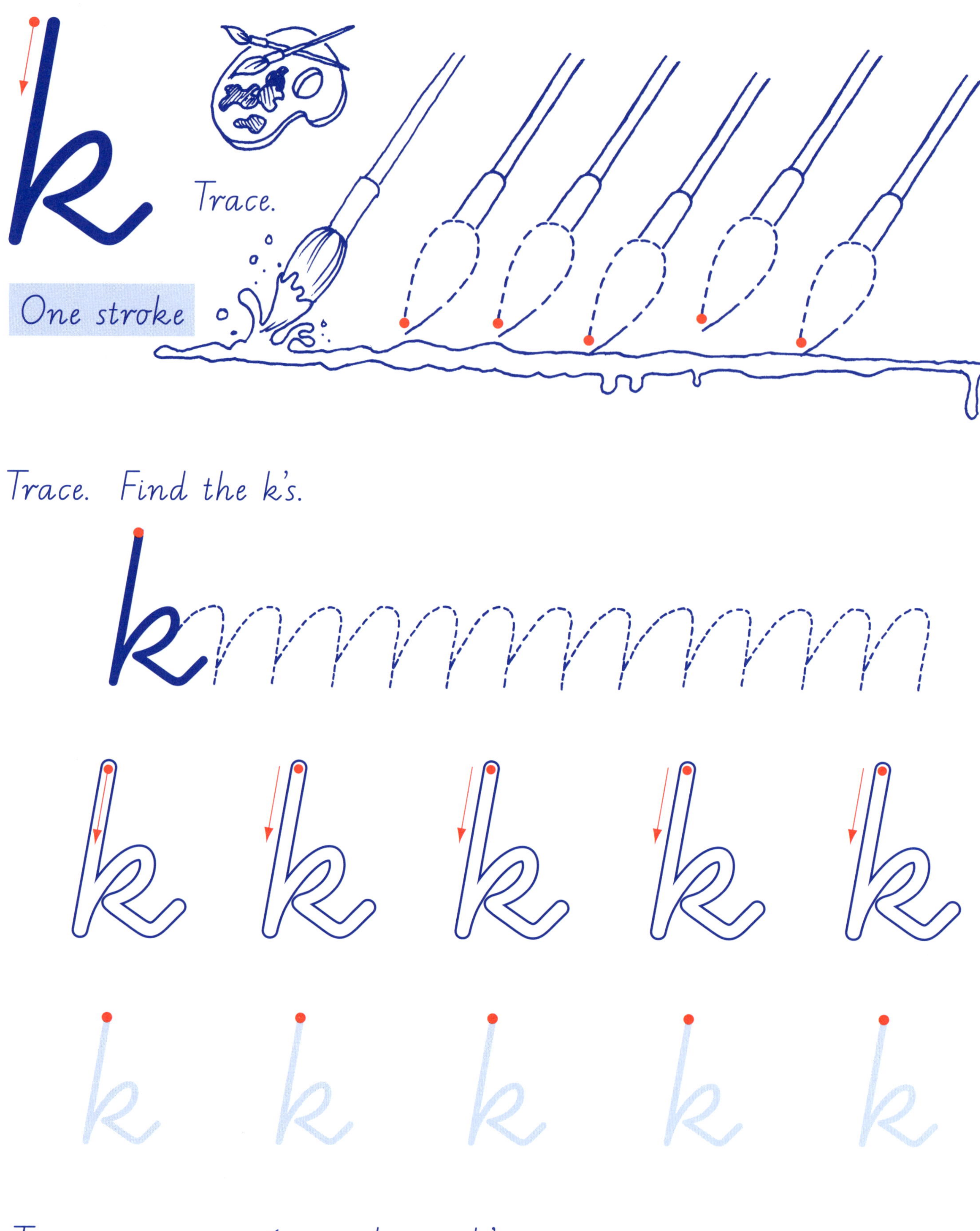

Try your own. ✓ your best 2 k's.

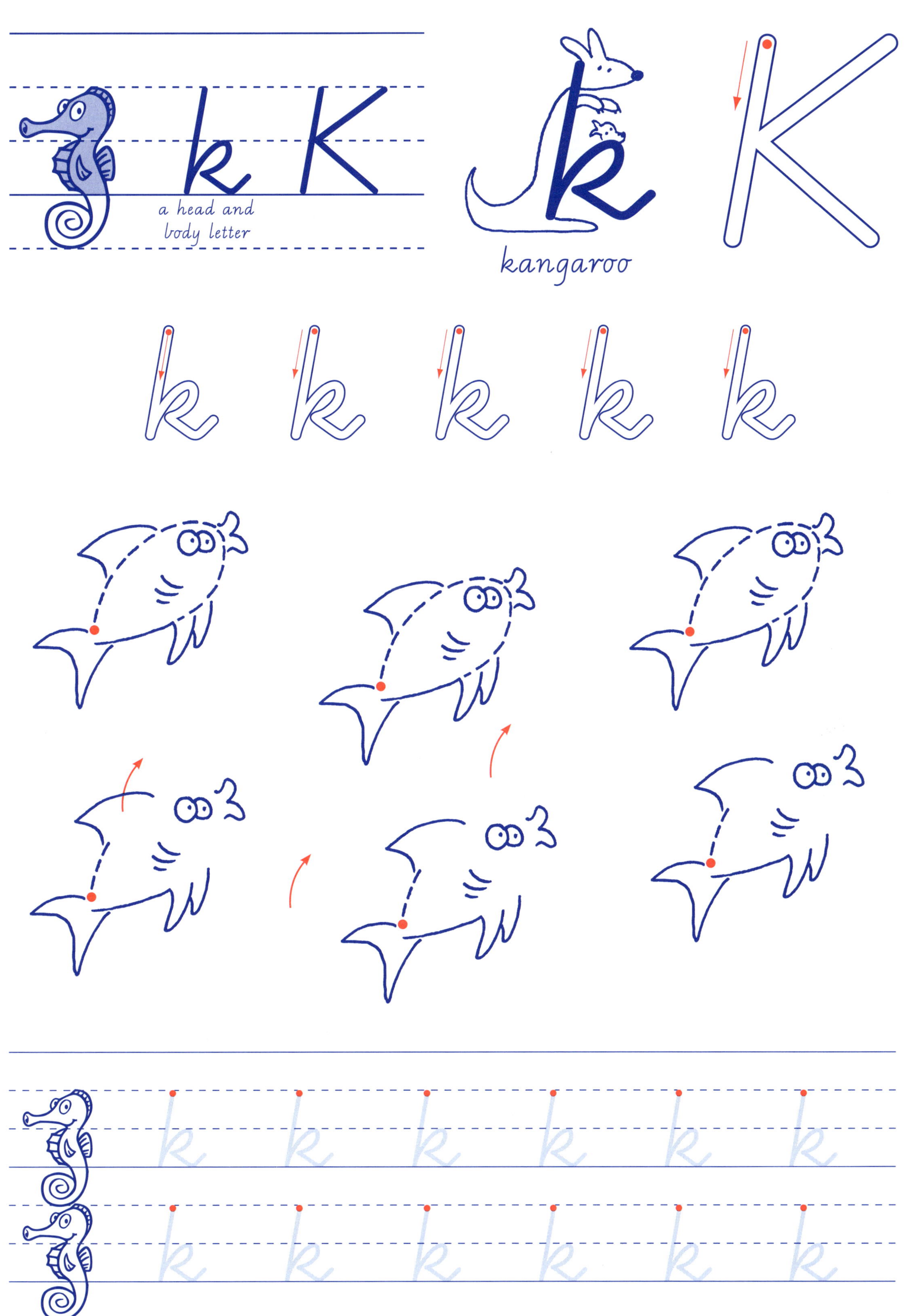

k K
a head and body letter
kangaroo

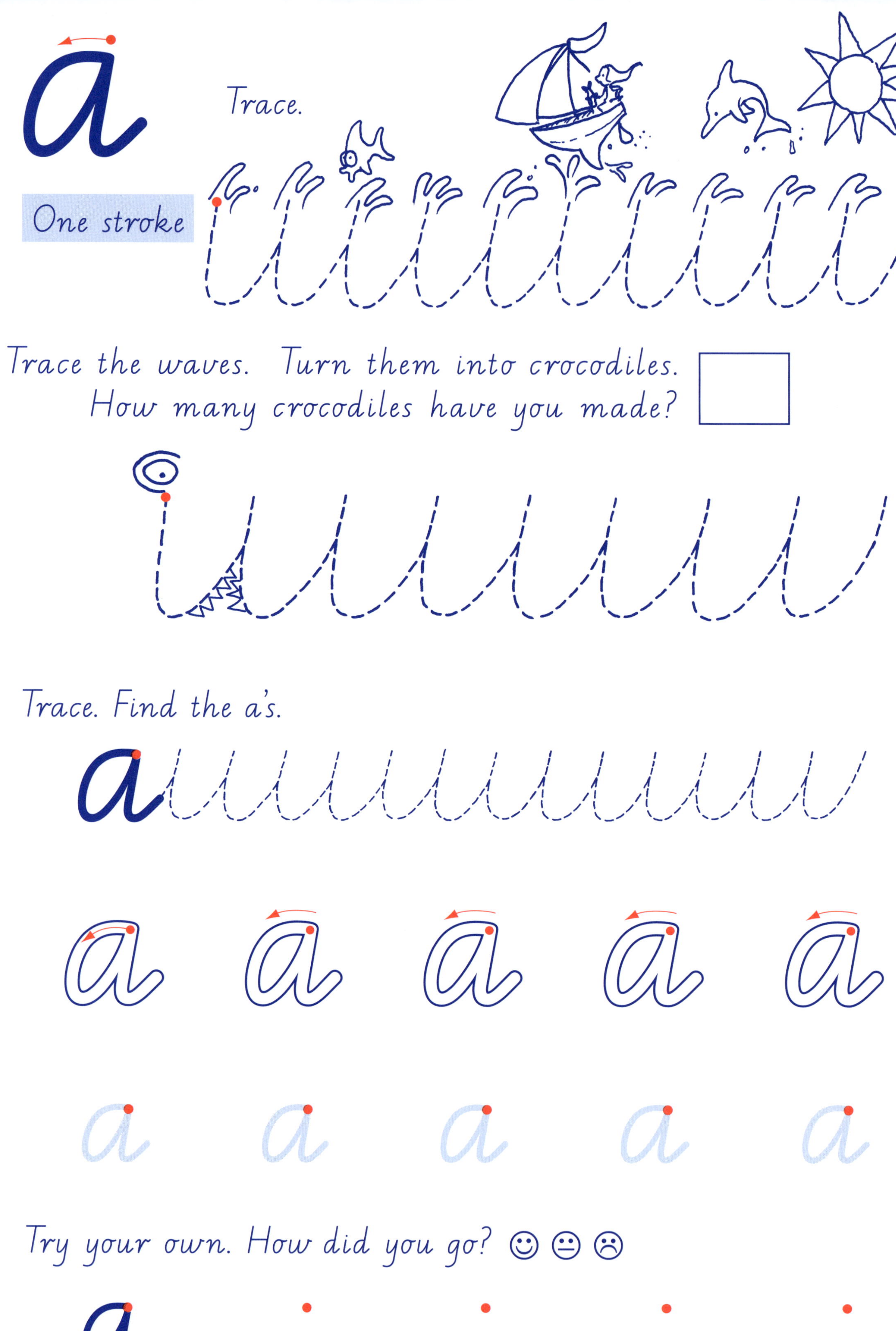
a
One stroke
Trace.
Trace the waves. Turn them into crocodiles.
How many crocodiles have you made?
Trace. Find the a's.
Try your own. How did you go?

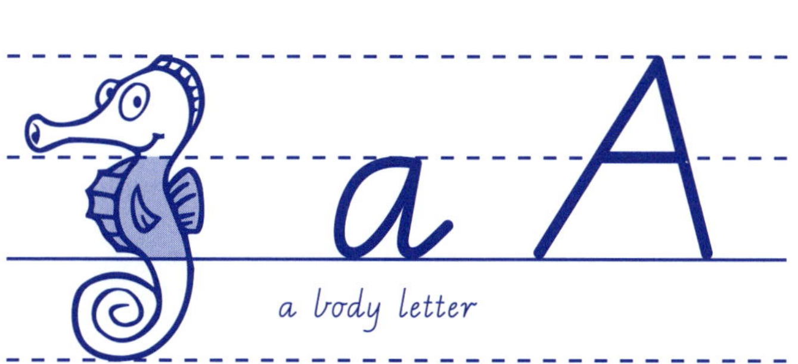

ant

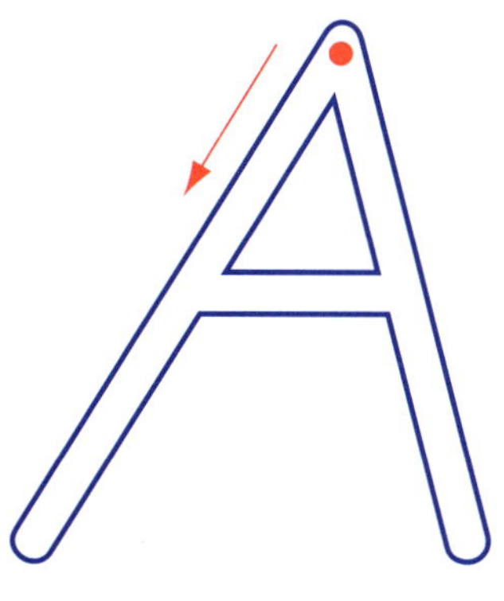

a a a a a

a a a a a a

a a a a a a

c

One stroke

Trace.

Use a crayon to trace the waves.

Trace. Find the c's.

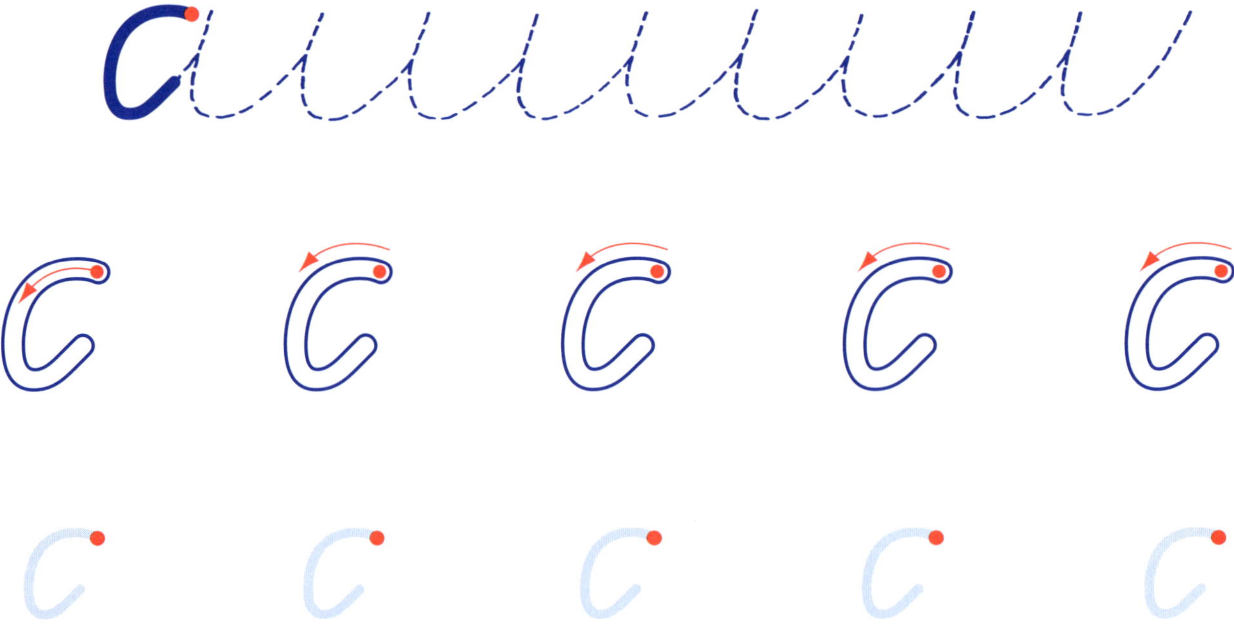

Try your own. Draw a inside your best c.

c

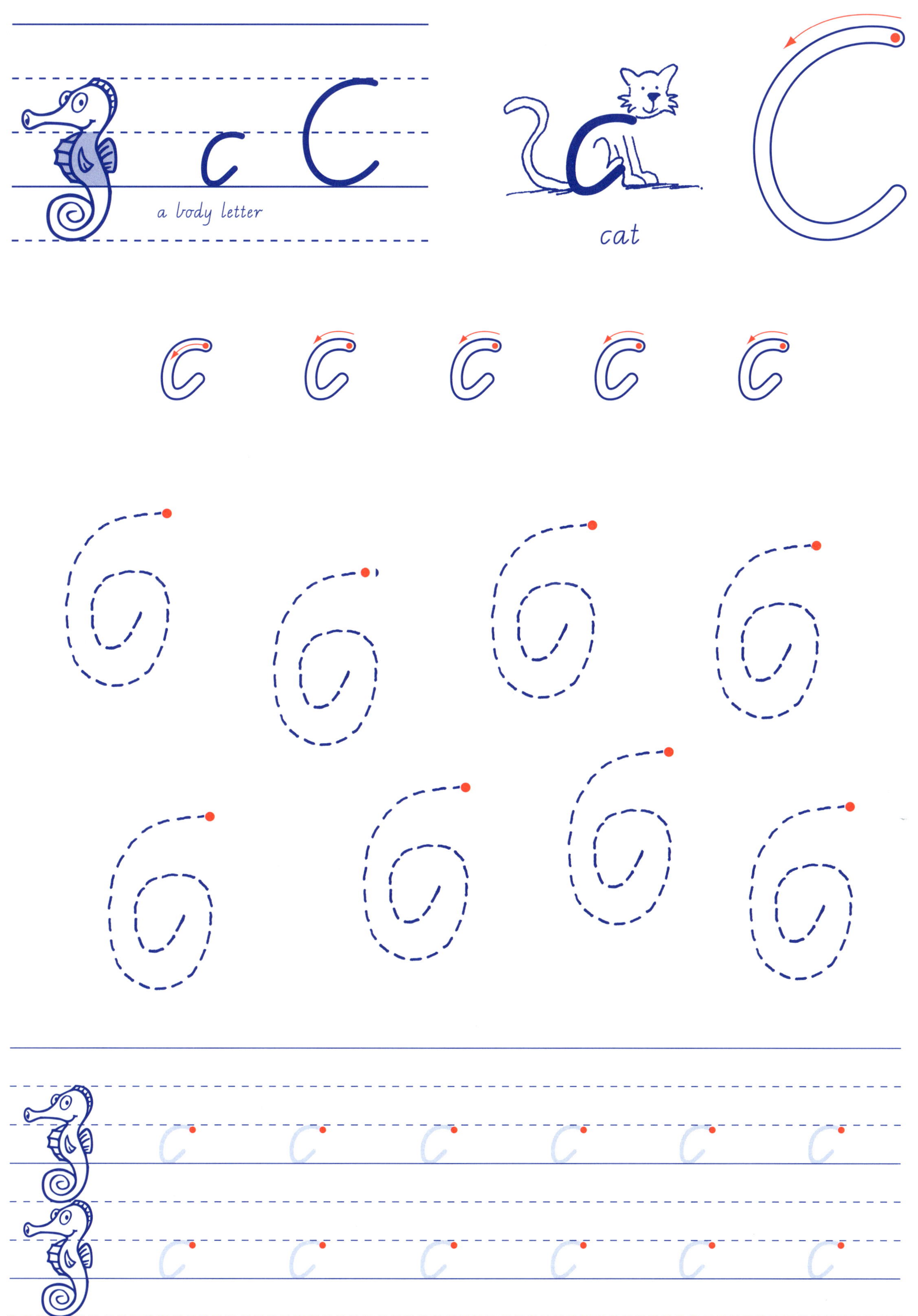

c C
a body letter
cat

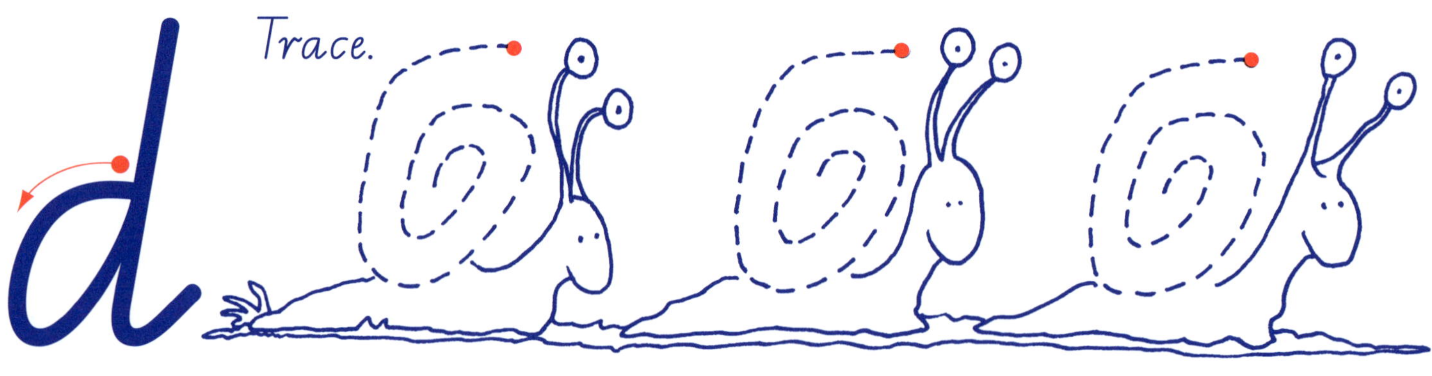

One stroke

Trace. Turn the waves into faces.

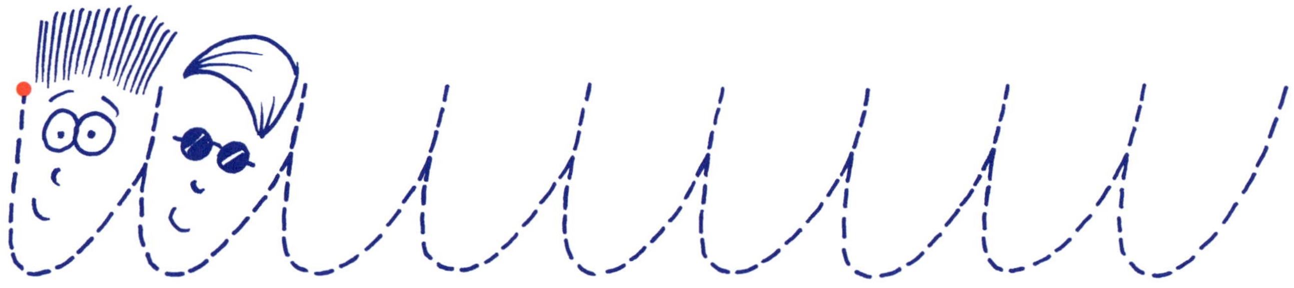

Trace. Find the d's.

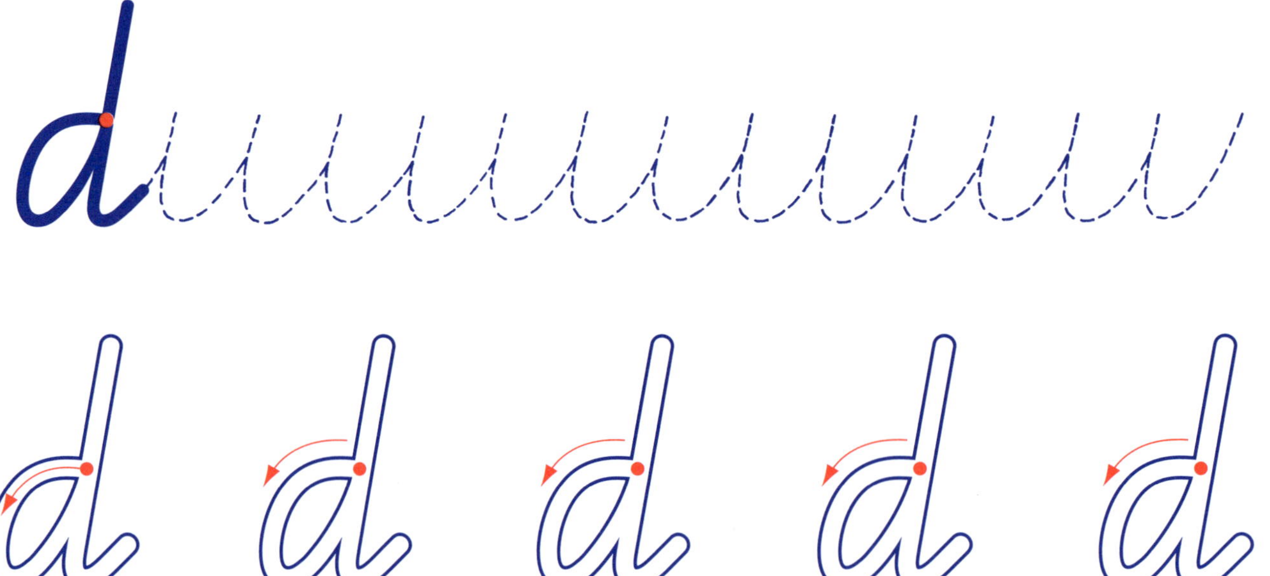

Try your own. Put a • inside your best d.

Does your friend agree? ☐ yes ☐ no

d

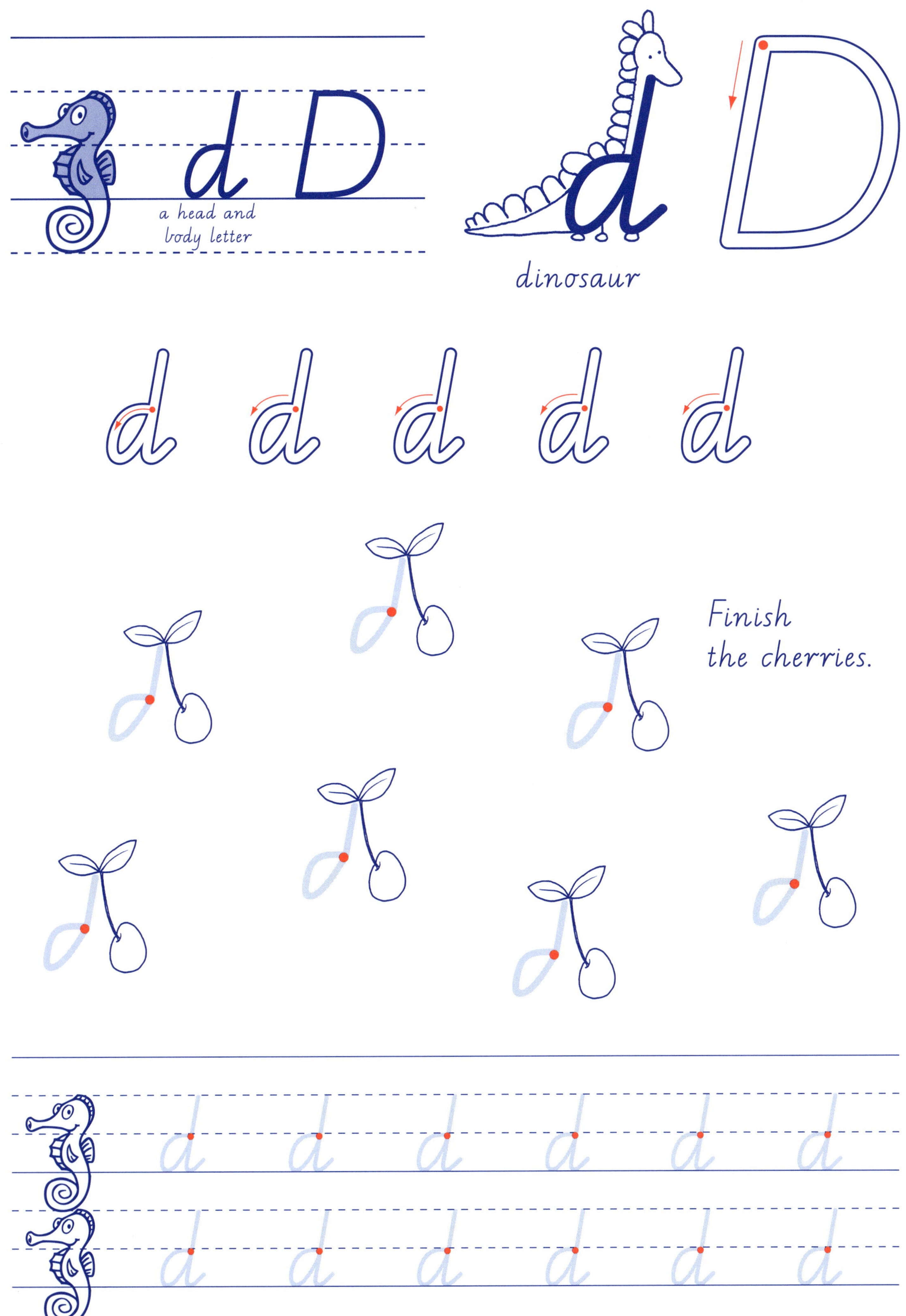

d D
a head and body letter
d D
dinosaur
Finish the cherries.

g

One stroke

Trace the waves with your fingers, then use a crayon to trace them.

Trace. Find the g's.

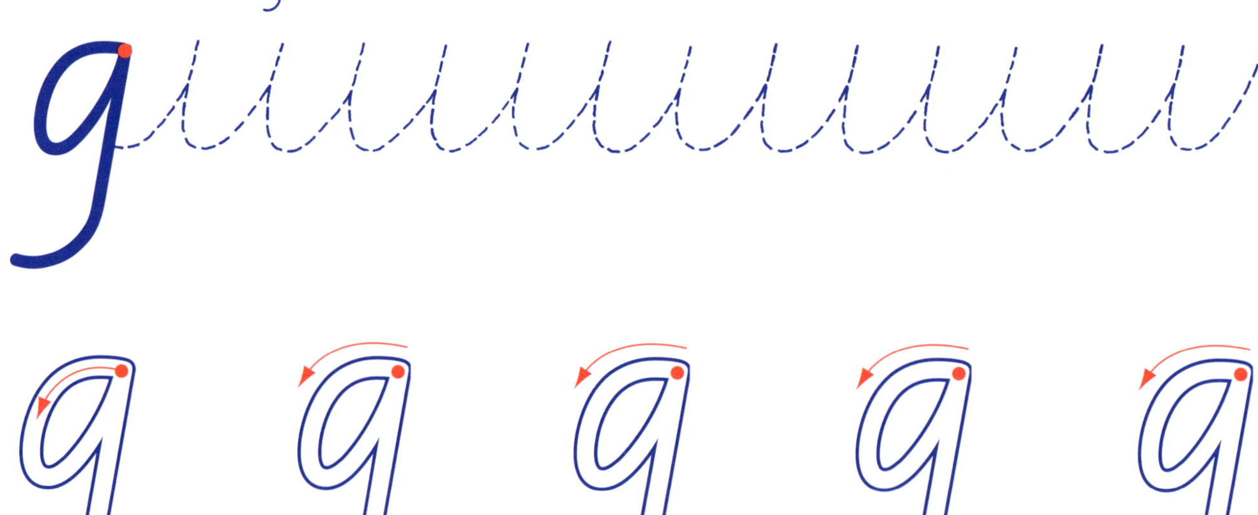

Try your own. Draw some ww under your best g.

g

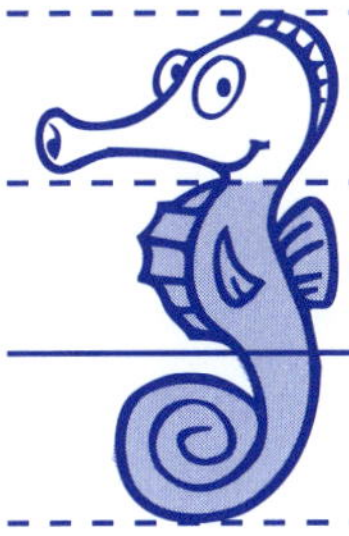

a body and tail letter

g G

goat

G

g g g g g

Finish the glasses.

g g g g g g

g g g g g g

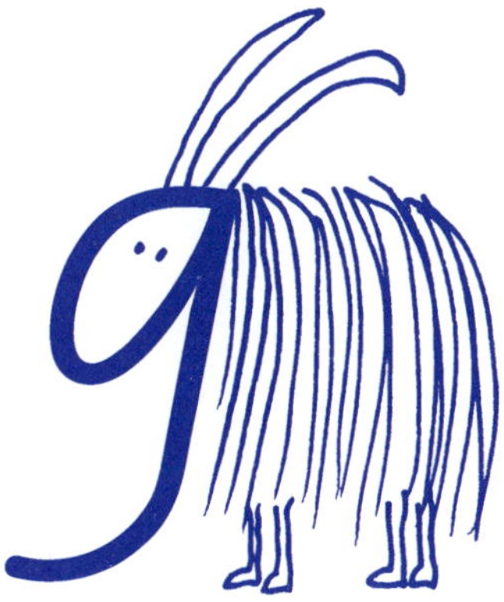

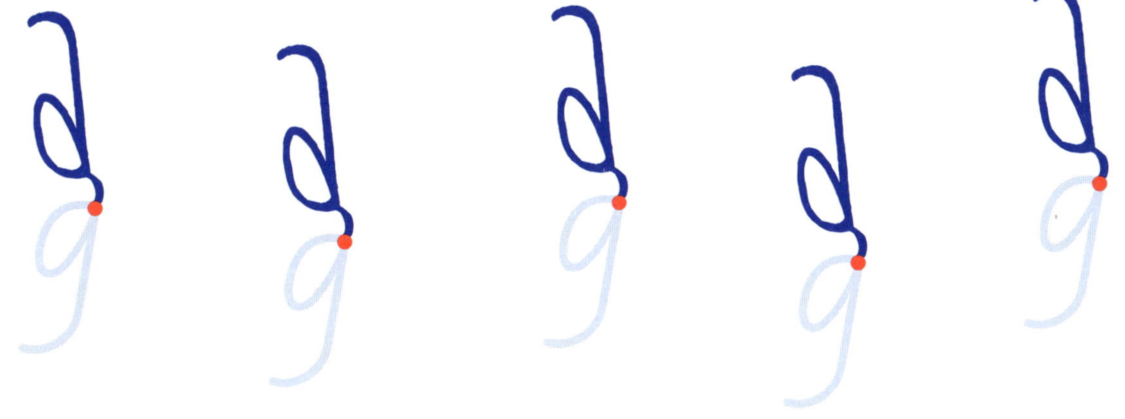

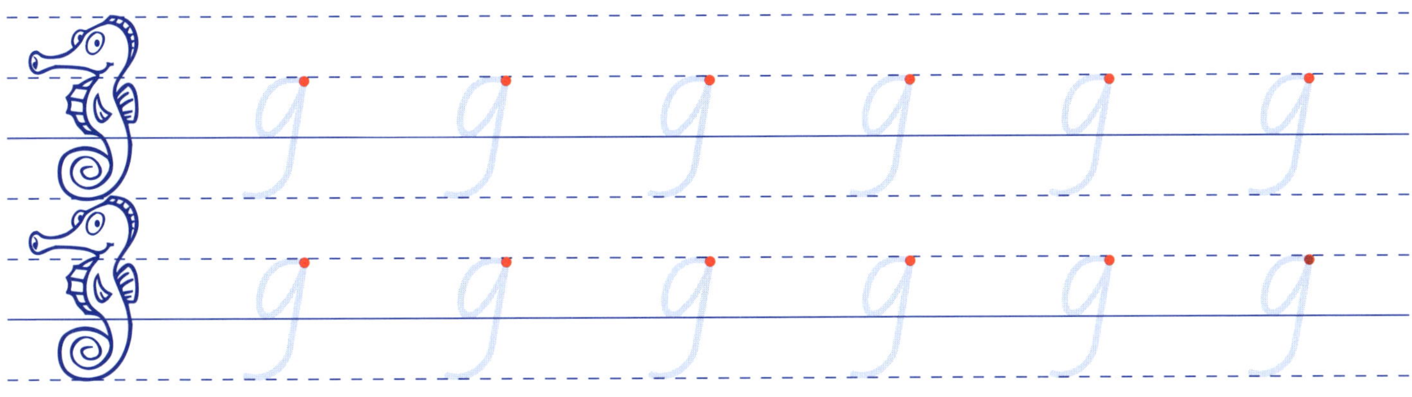

q

Track.

One stroke

Trace the waves. Turn every second wave into a duck.
How many have you made?

Trace. Find the q's.

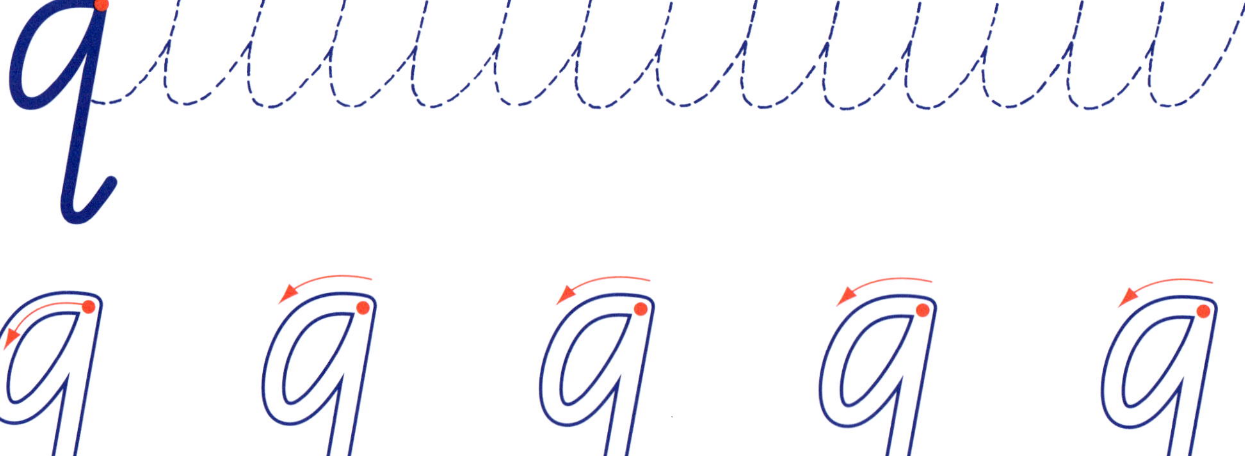

Try your own. Tick the box if all your q's have a tail and a flick.

q

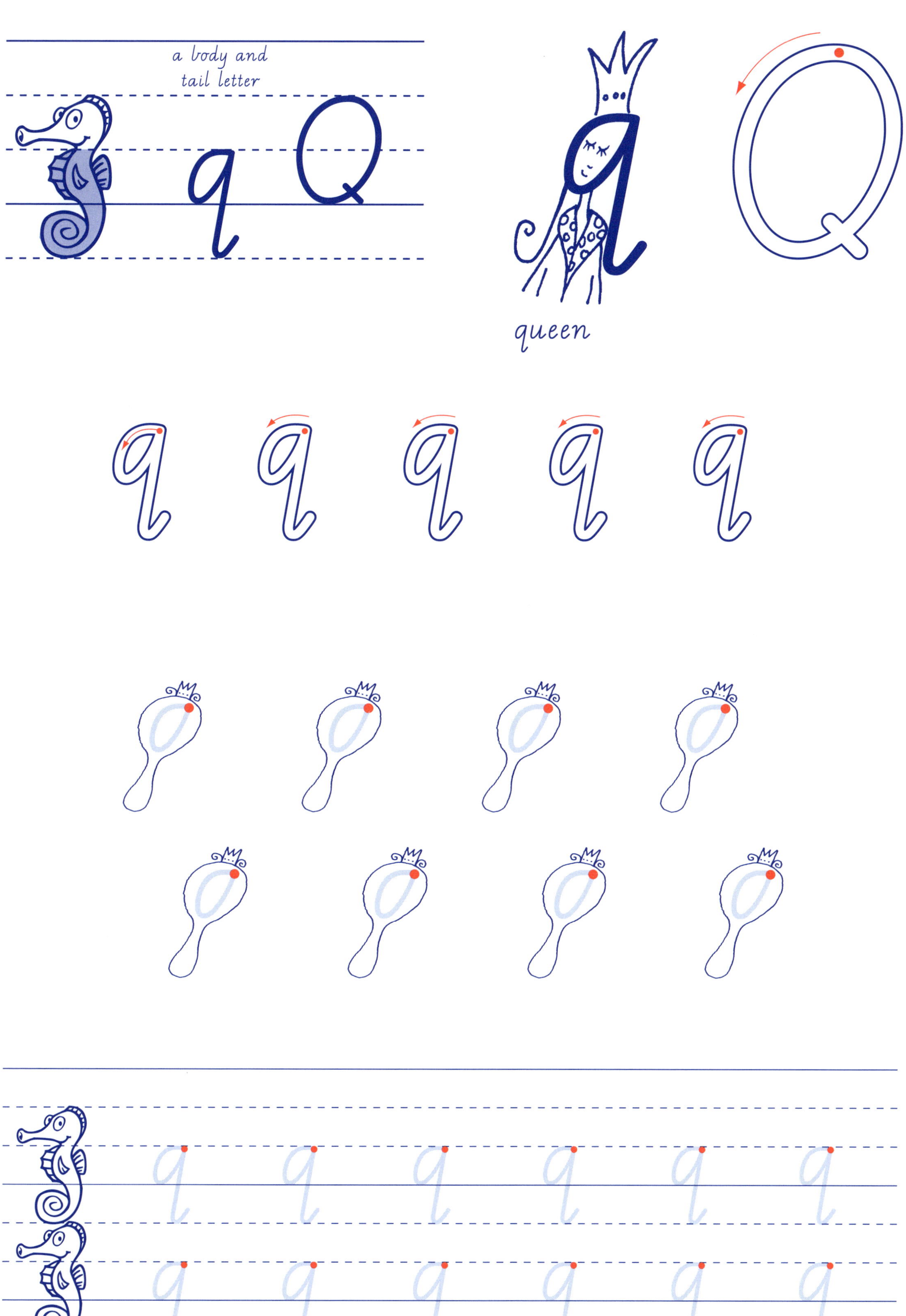
a body and
tail letter
q Q
queen

One stroke

Trace.

Trace. Now turn the waves into your own mice.

Trace. Find the o's.

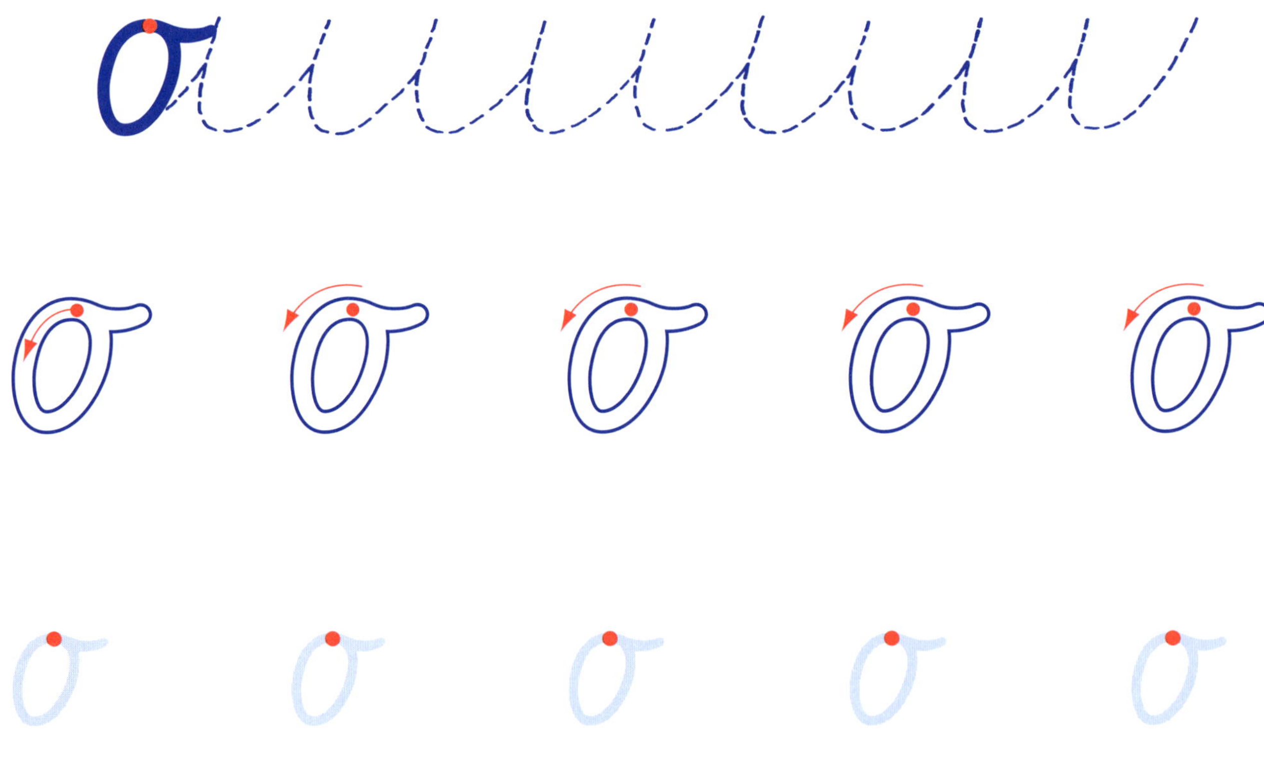

Try your own. Are your o's okay?

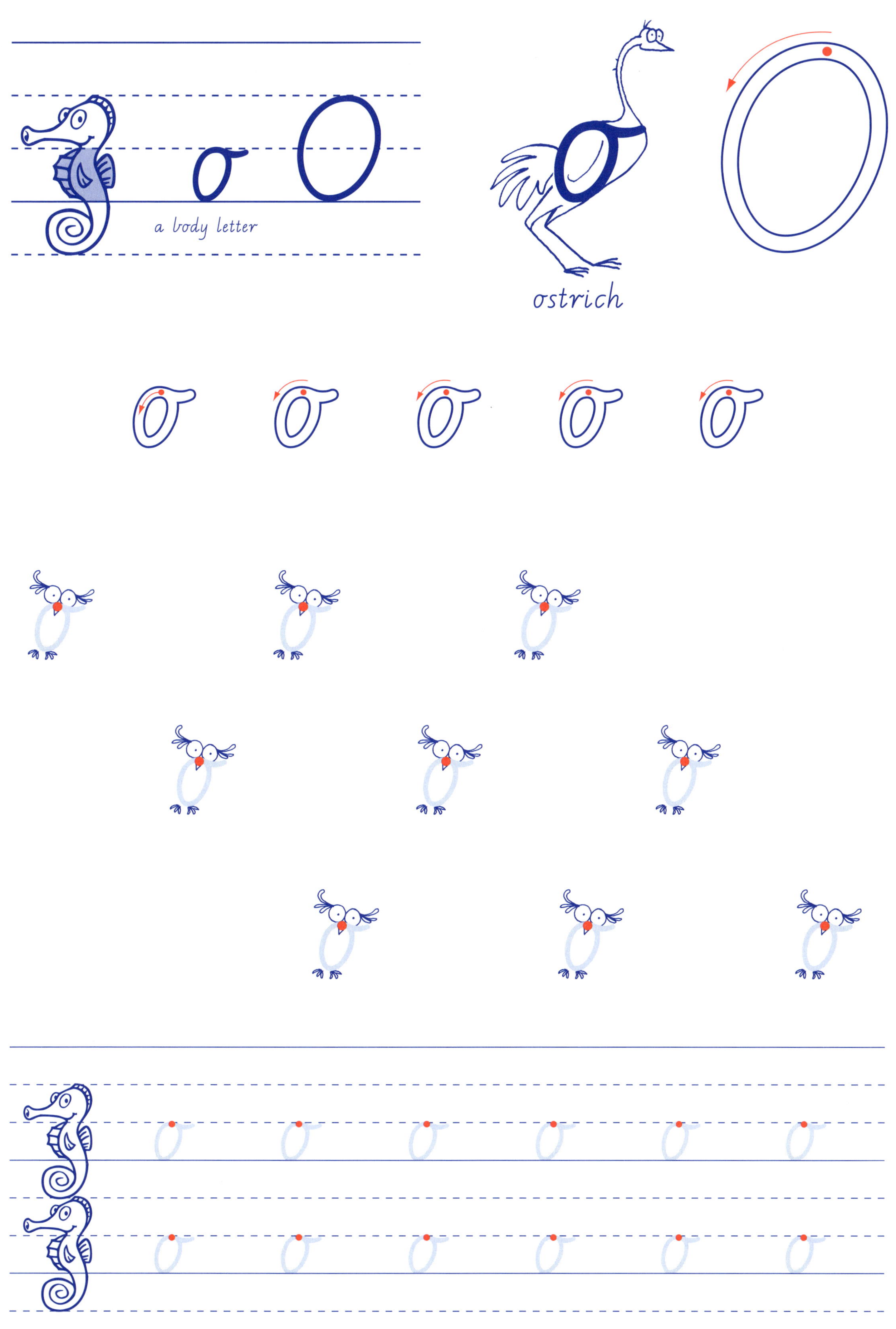
a body letter
ostrich

e

Trace.

One stroke

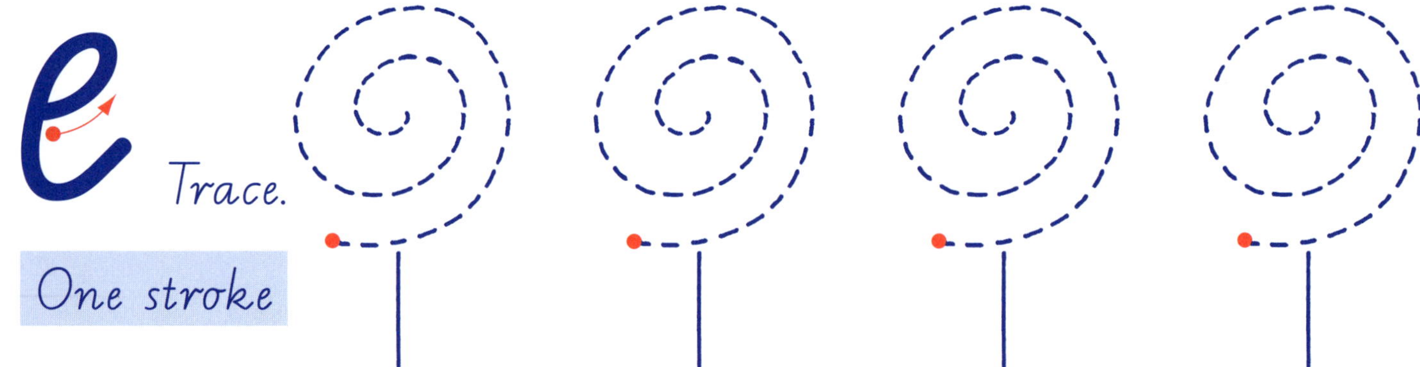

Trace. Colour the wedges.

Trace. Find the e's.

Try your own. How did you do? ☺ 😐 ☹

e

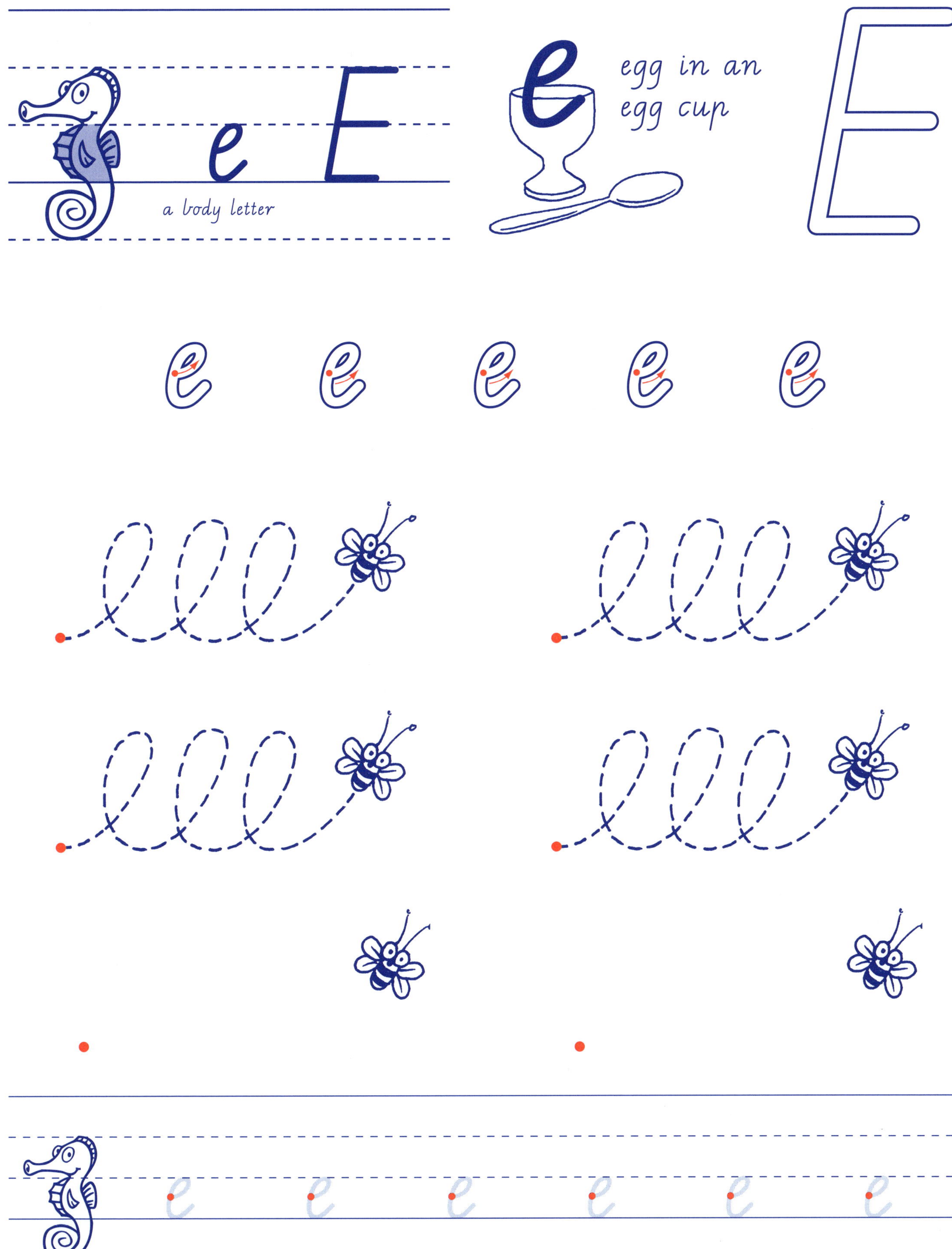
e E
a body letter
e
egg in an
egg cup
E

Trace.

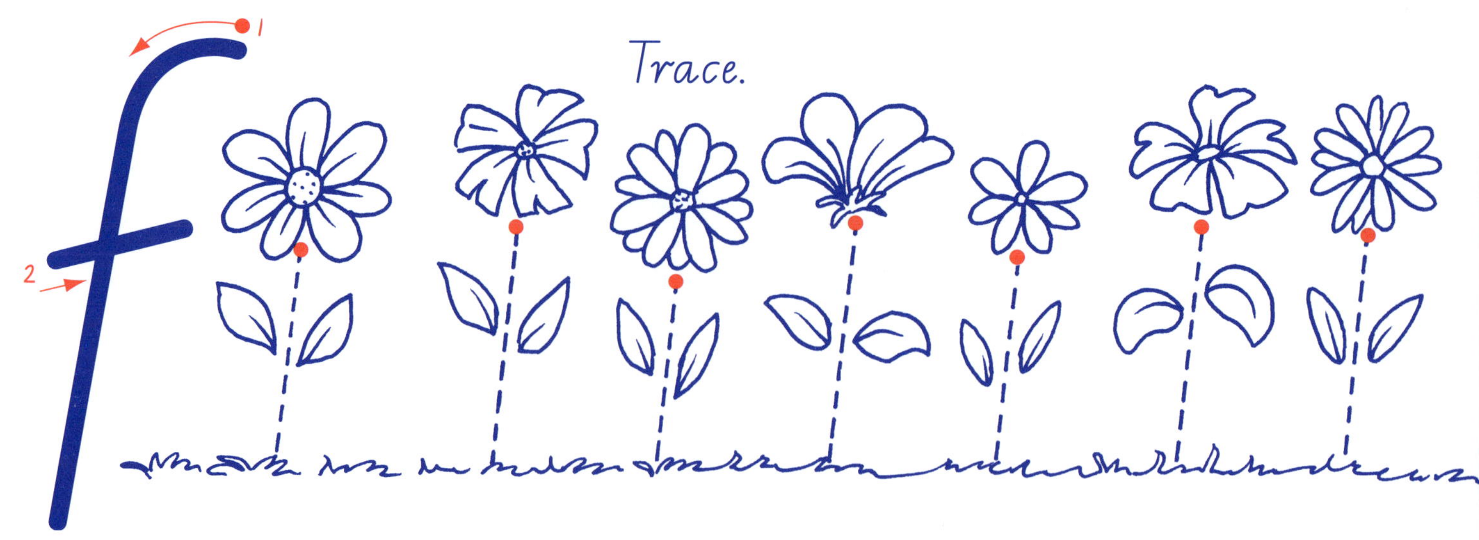

Two strokes

Find f.

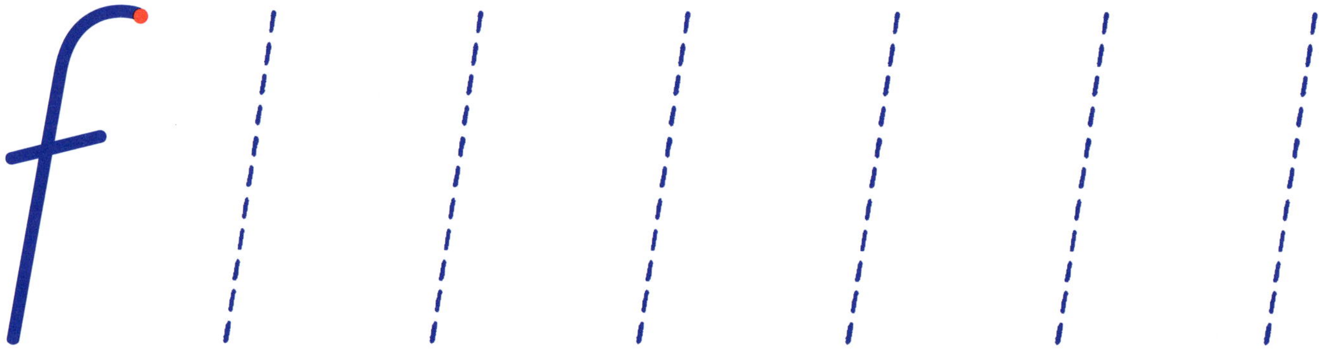

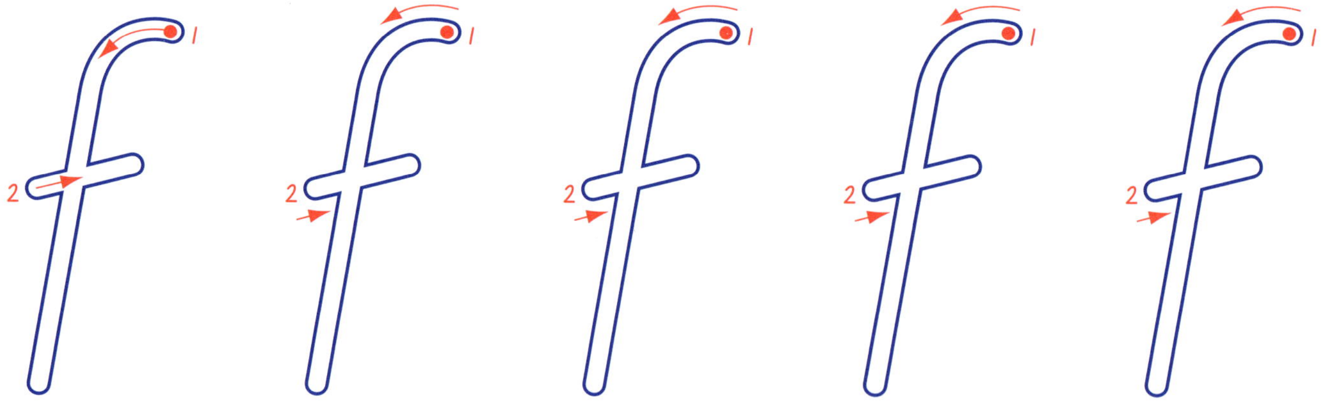

Try your own. Draw a fish below your best f.

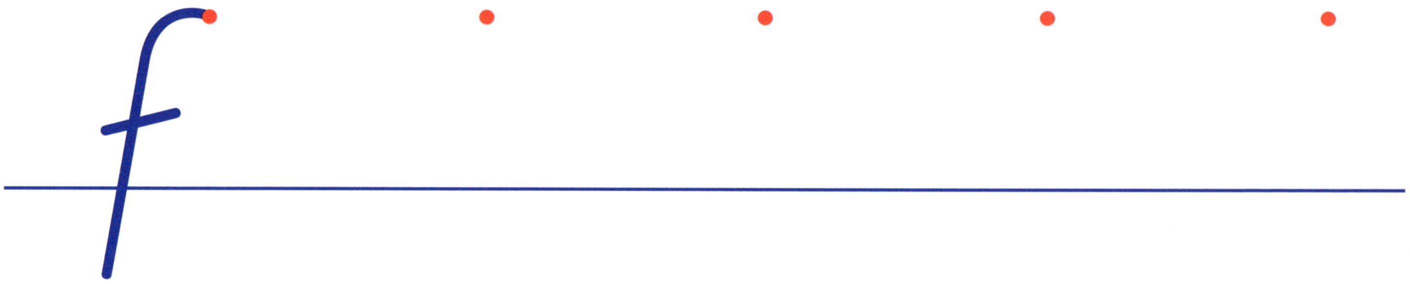

Trace Grandad's walking stick.

s

One stroke

Trace.

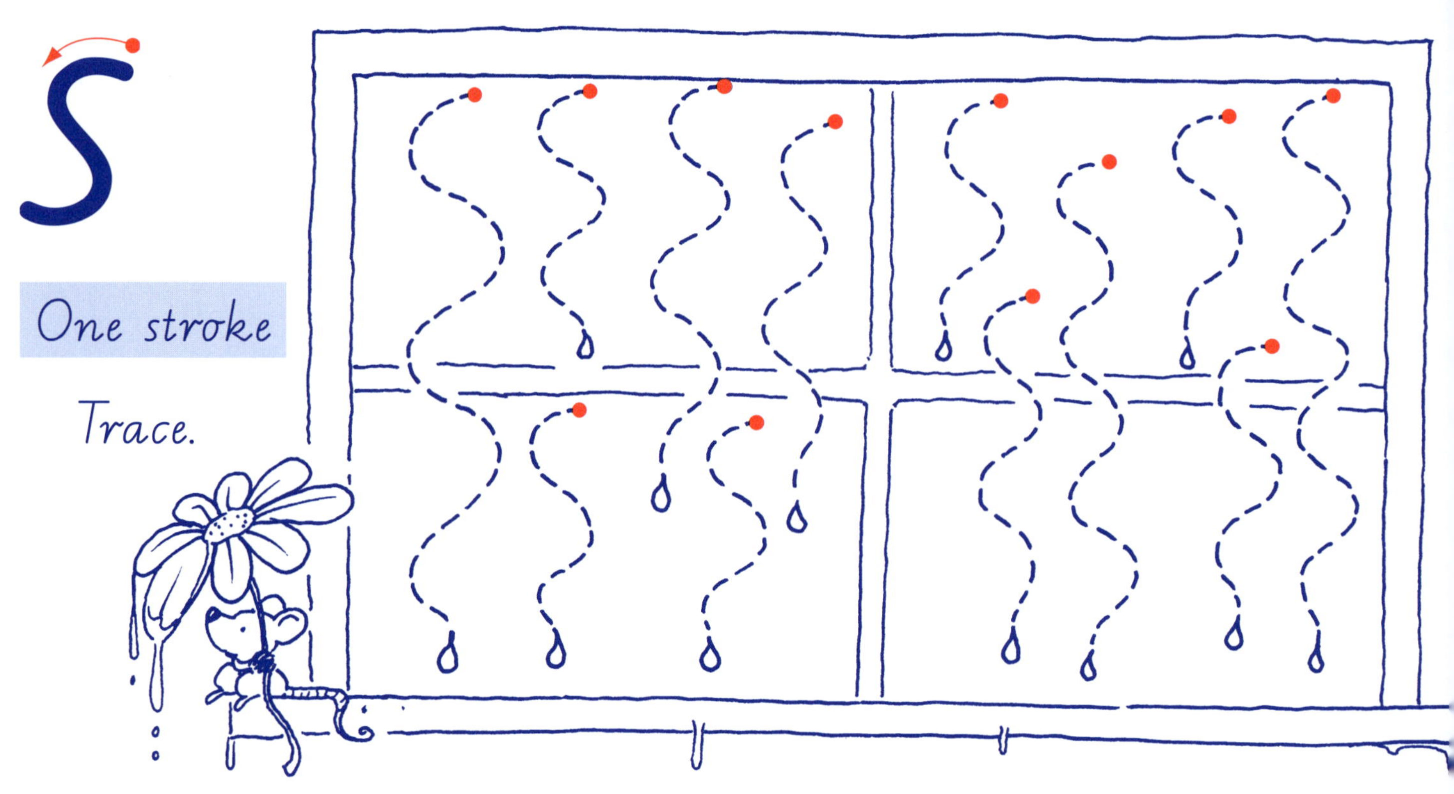

Trace. Find the s's.

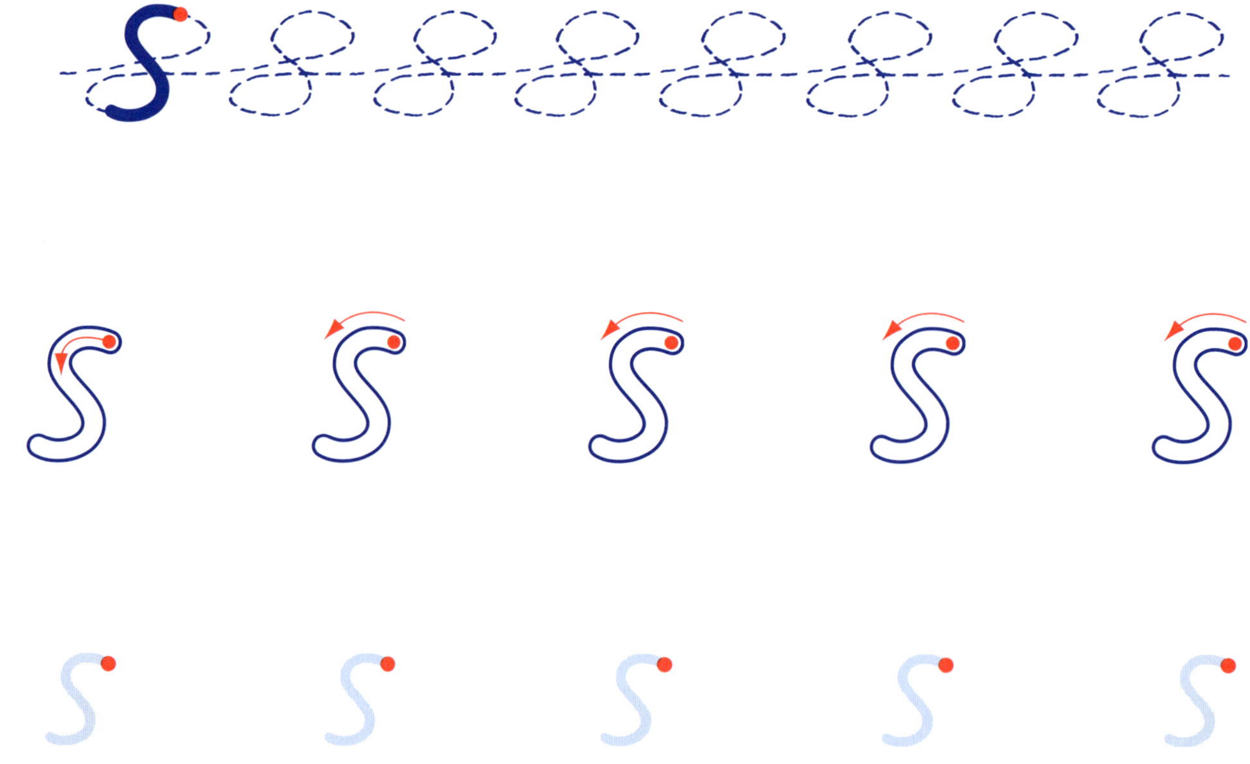

Try your own. Draw a squiggle under your best s.

s

s S
a body letter
snake

u

One stroke

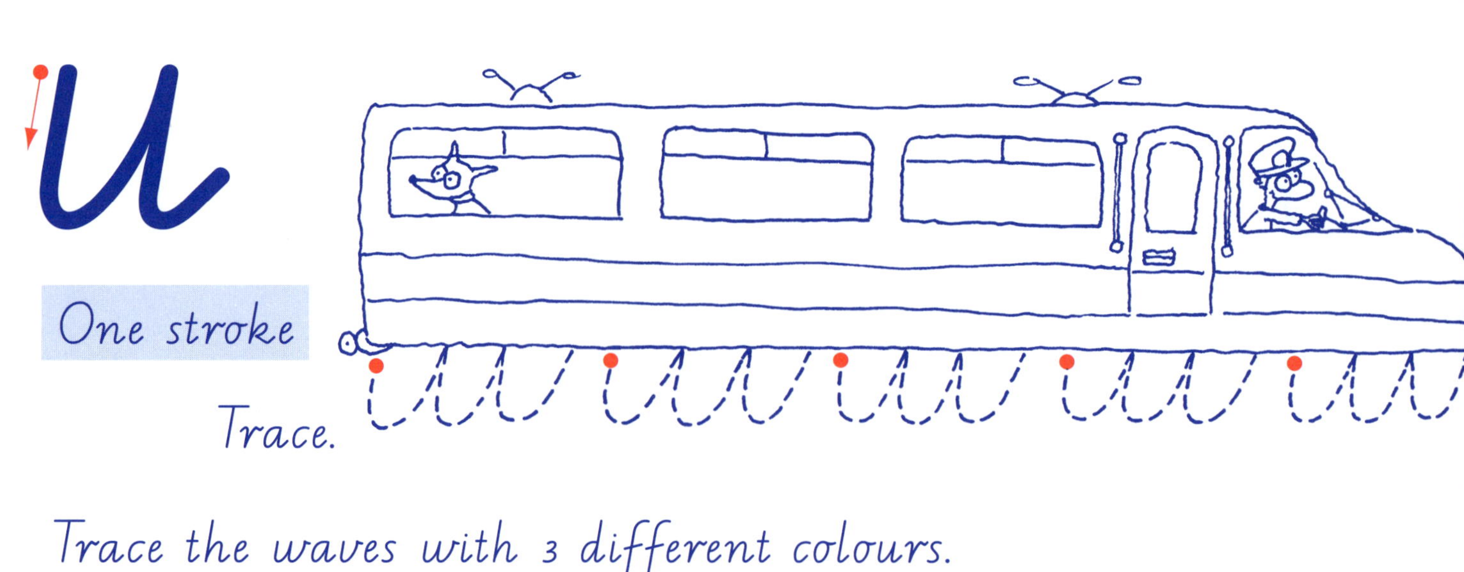

Trace.

Trace the waves with 3 different colours.

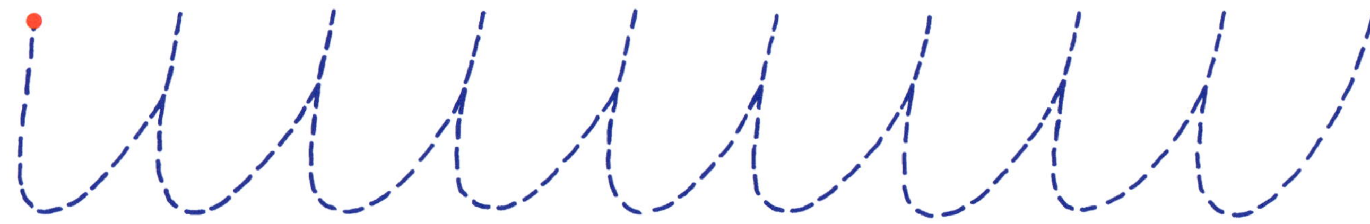

Trace. Find the u's.

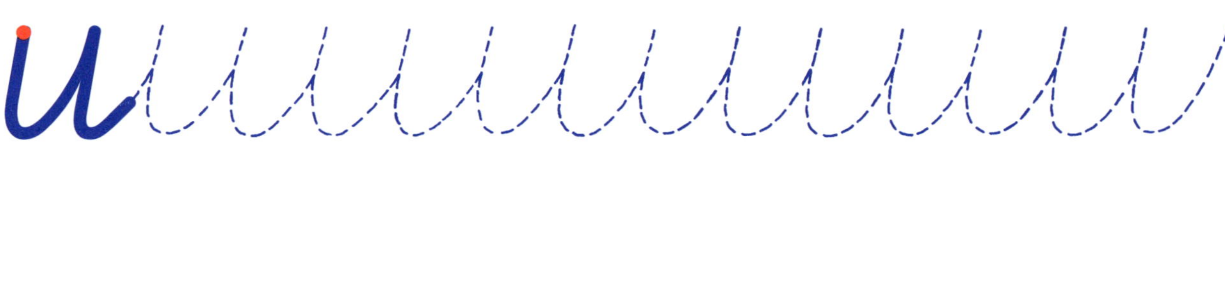

Try your own. Do all your u's have a wedge? ☐ yes ☐ no

u

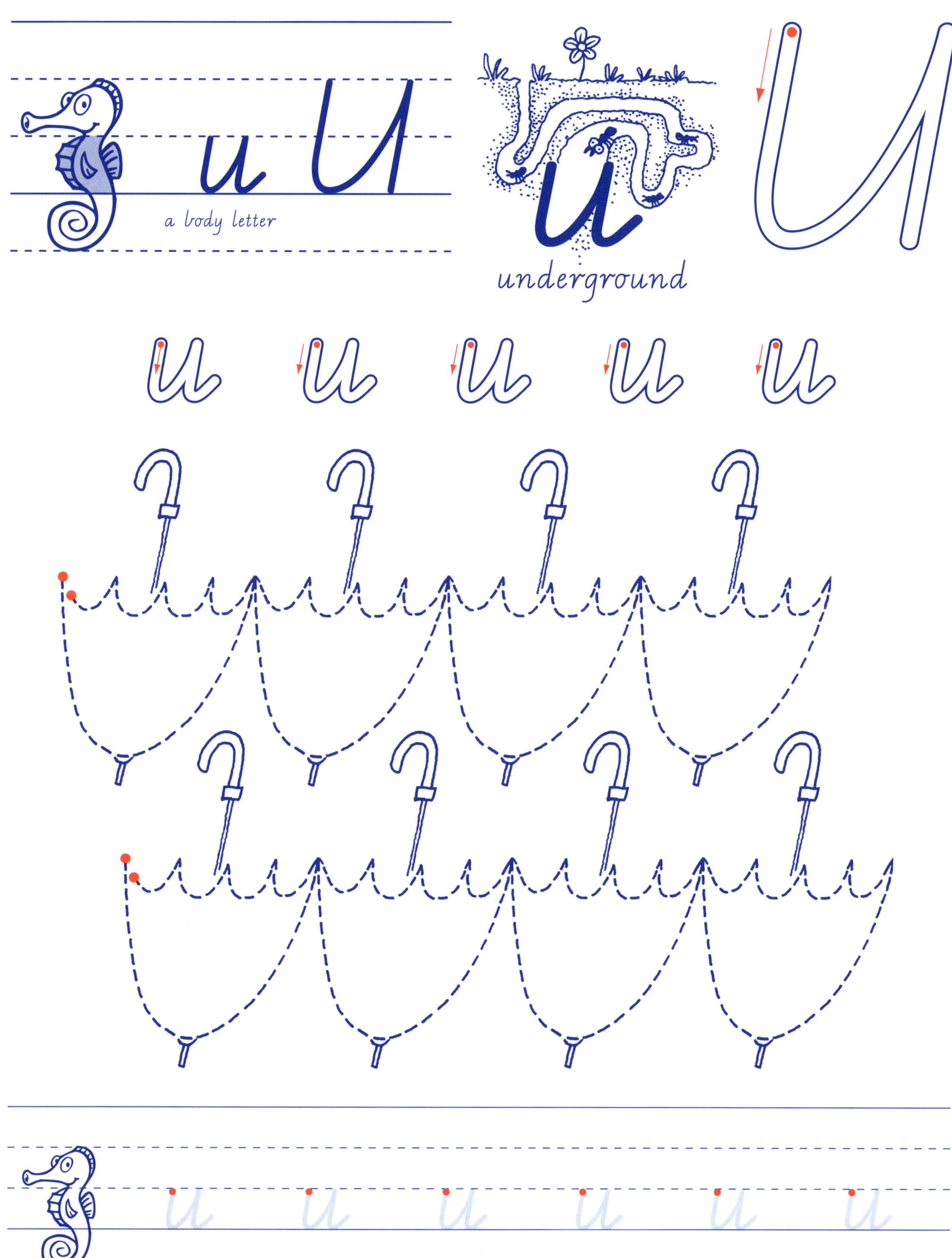
u U
a body letter
u
underground
U
u u u u u

y

Trace.

One stroke

Track.

Trace. Find the y's.

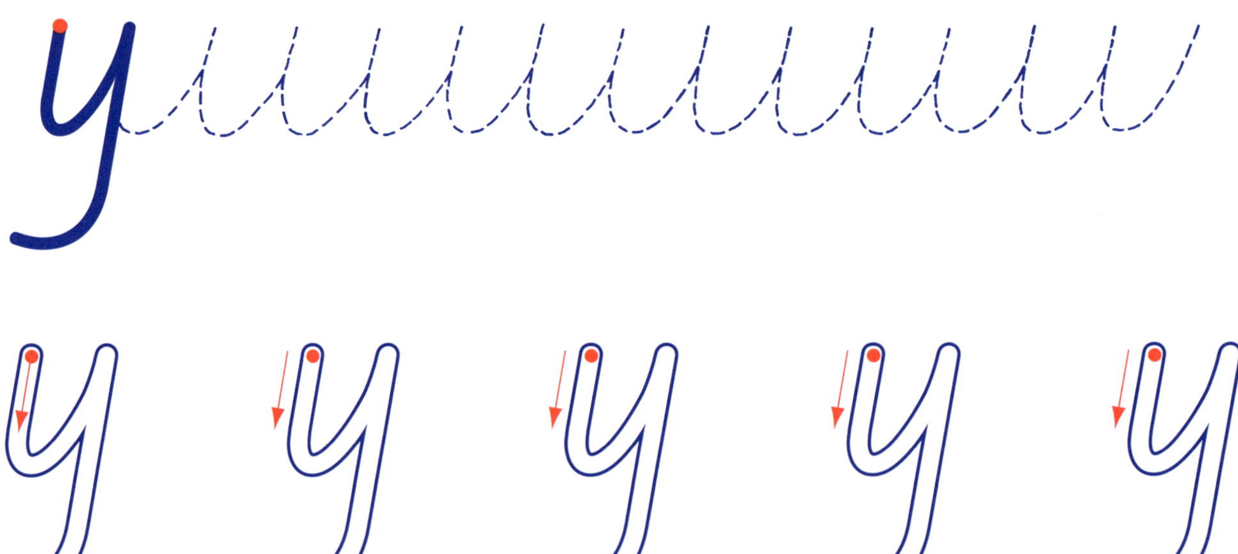

Try your own. Draw a ✳ on the y with the best tail.

y

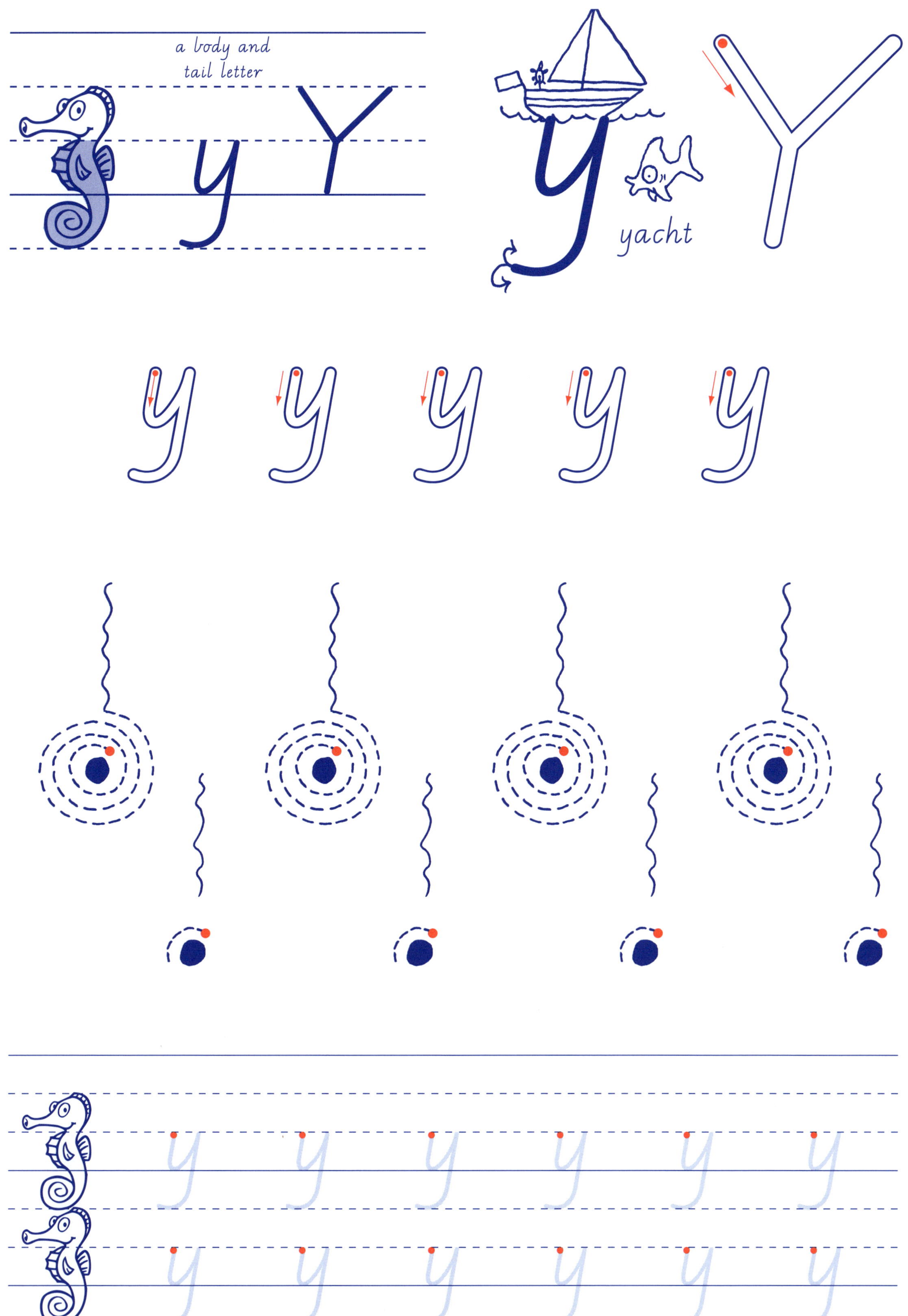
a body and
tail letter
y Y
y
yacht
Y

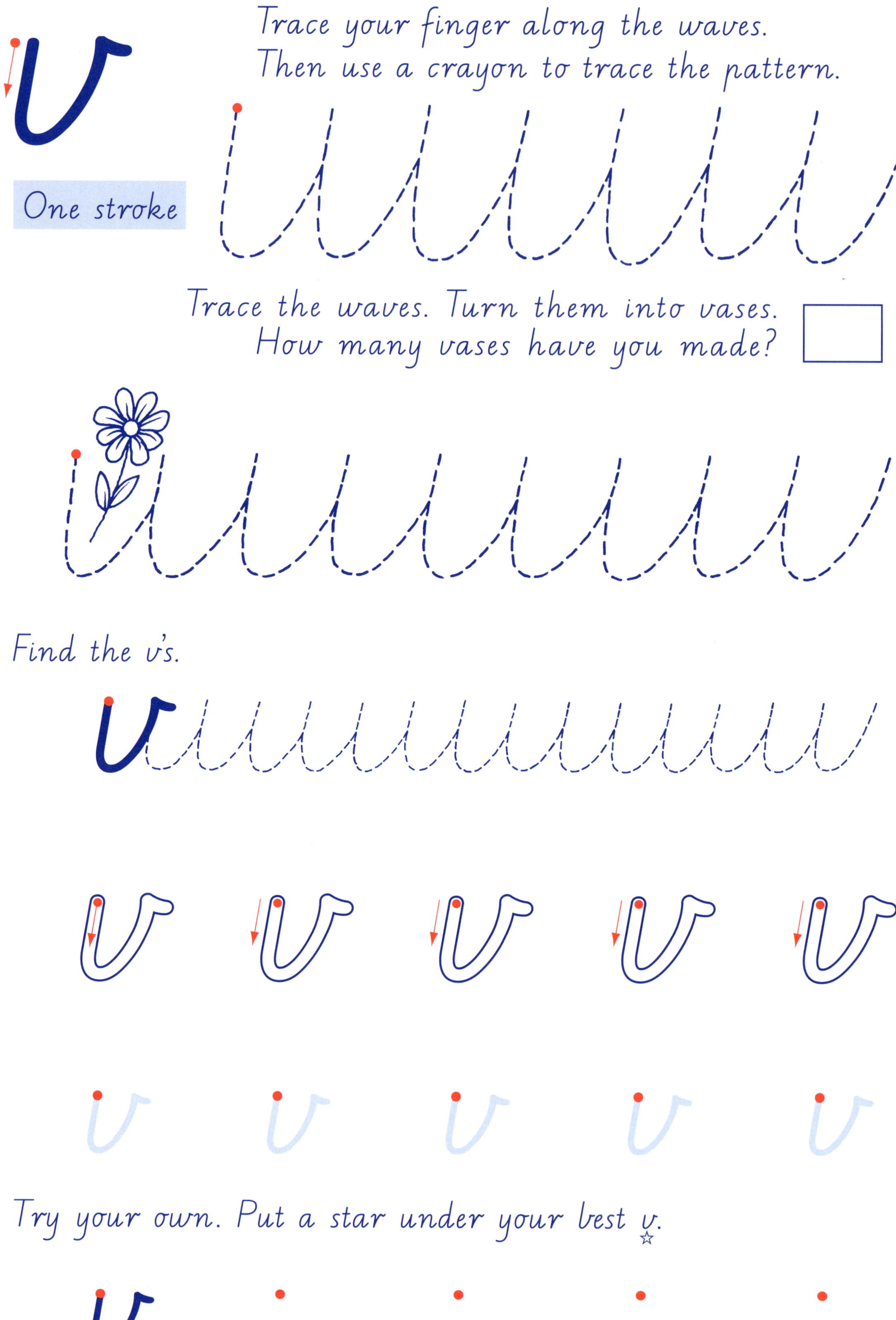

Try your own. Put a star under your best v.

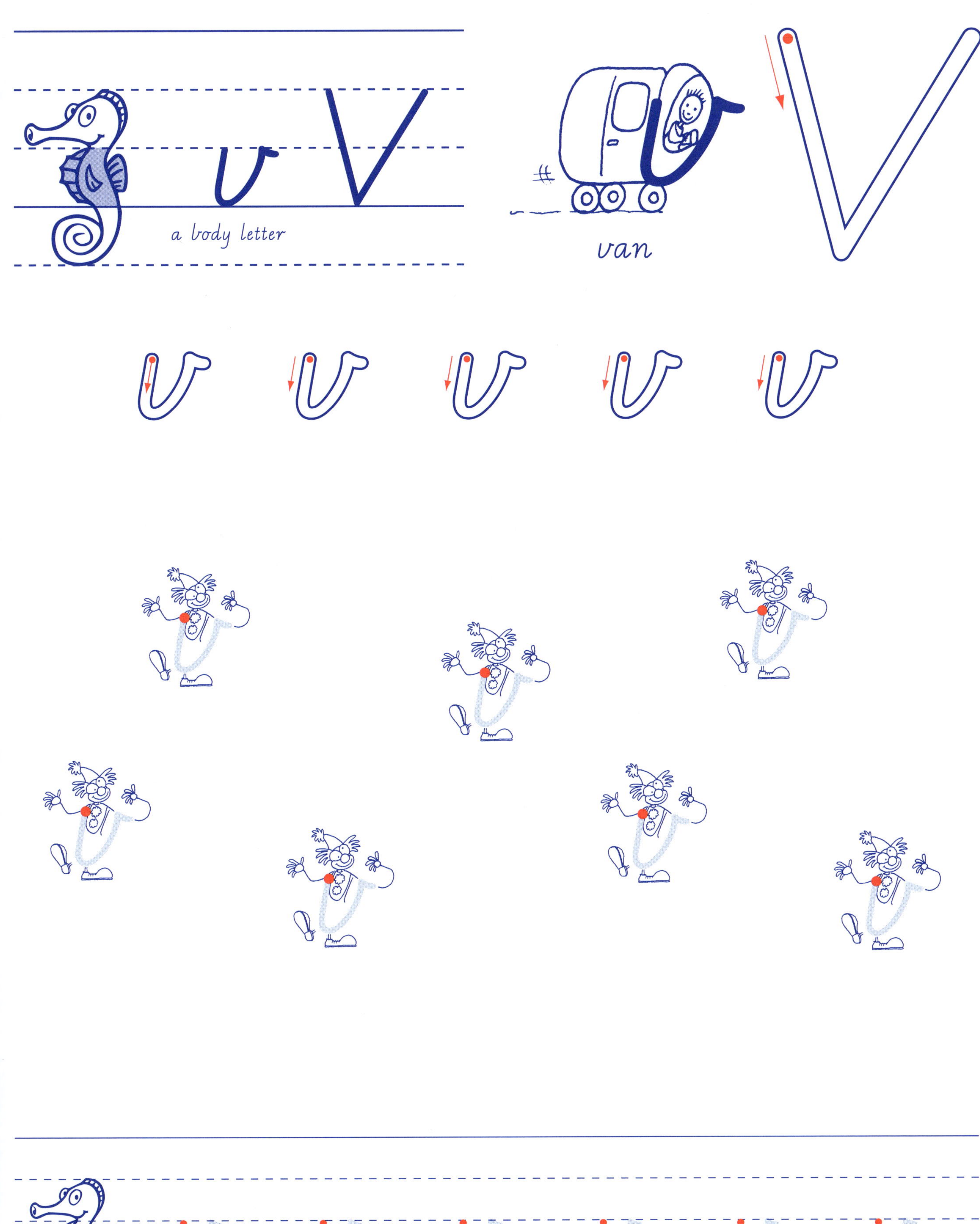
a body letter
van

w

One stroke

Trace. Colour the wedges of cake.

Find the w's.

Try your own. ✓ your best w. Circle the (w) you think could be better

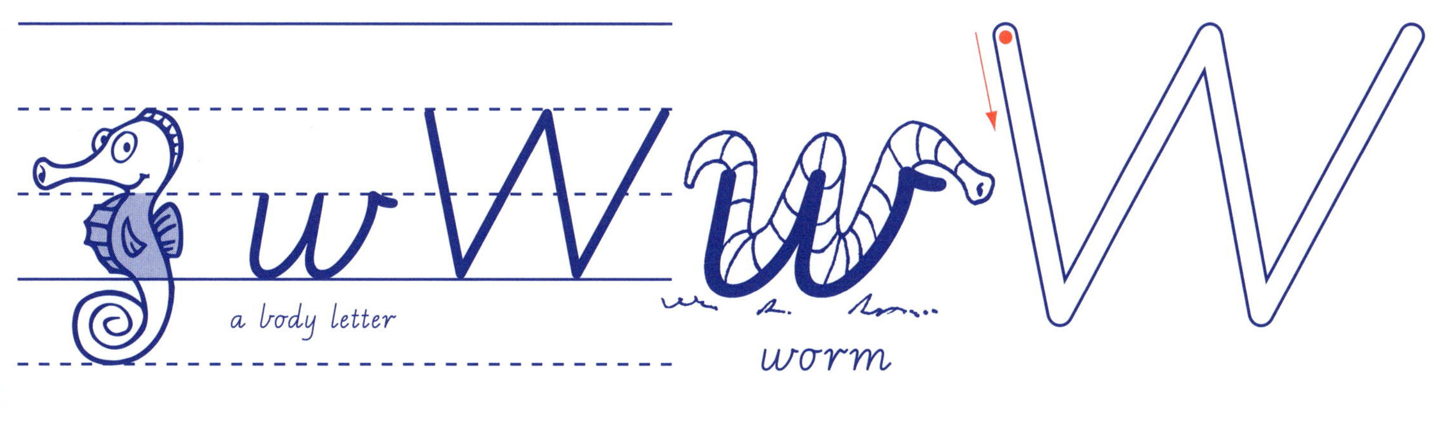
a body letter
worm

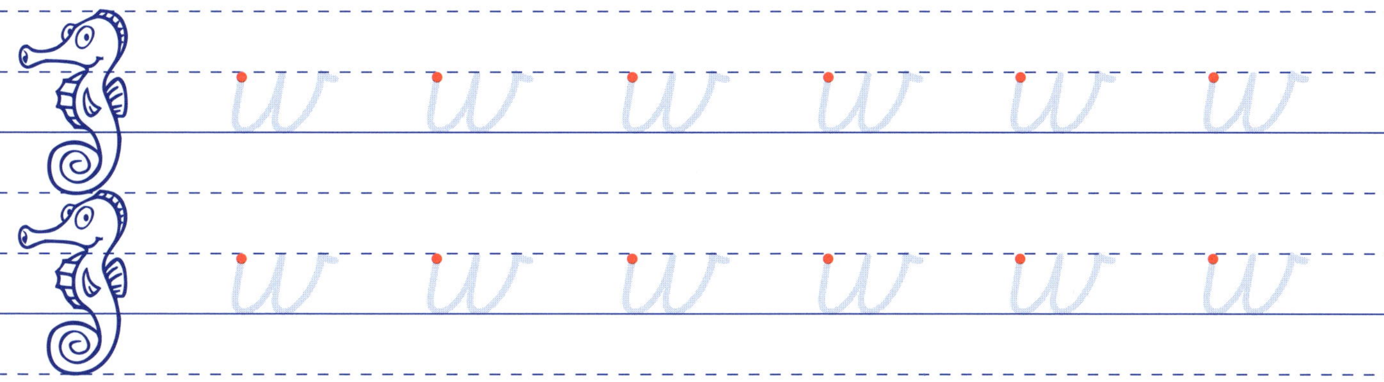

Use a crayon to trace the waves.

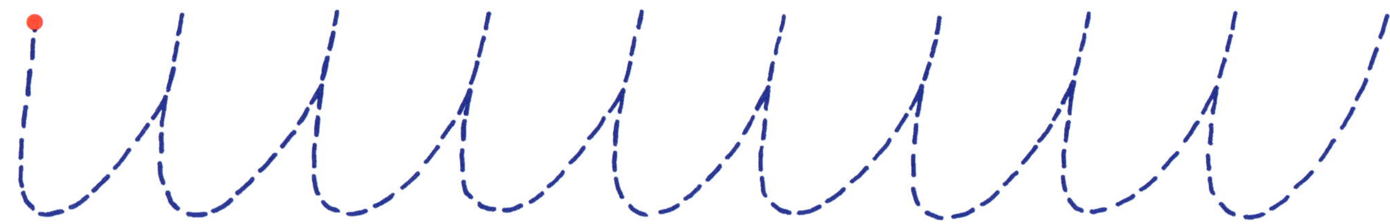

Trace. Find the b's.

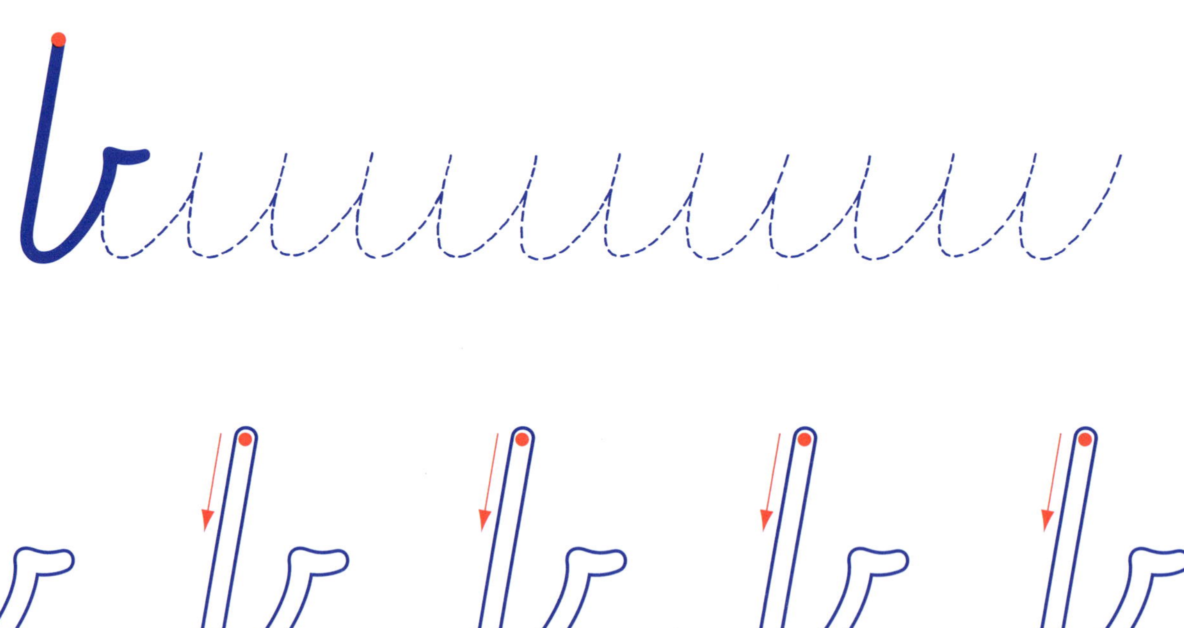

Try your own. Draw a box around your best b.

b B
a head and
body letter
bbb bbb
beetle
B

one sun

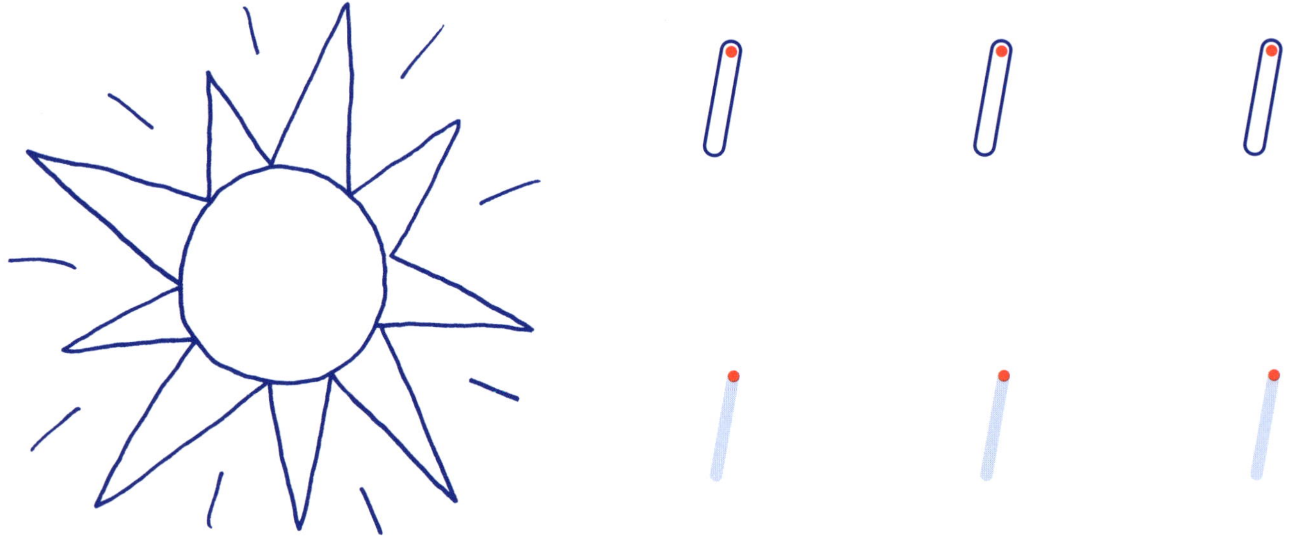

two wheels

Draw 2 ✱✱ under your best 2.

three children on a see-saw

four legs on a giraffe

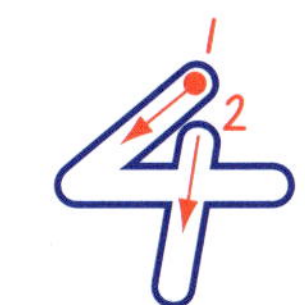   

Put a box around your best 4.

five rings on a hand

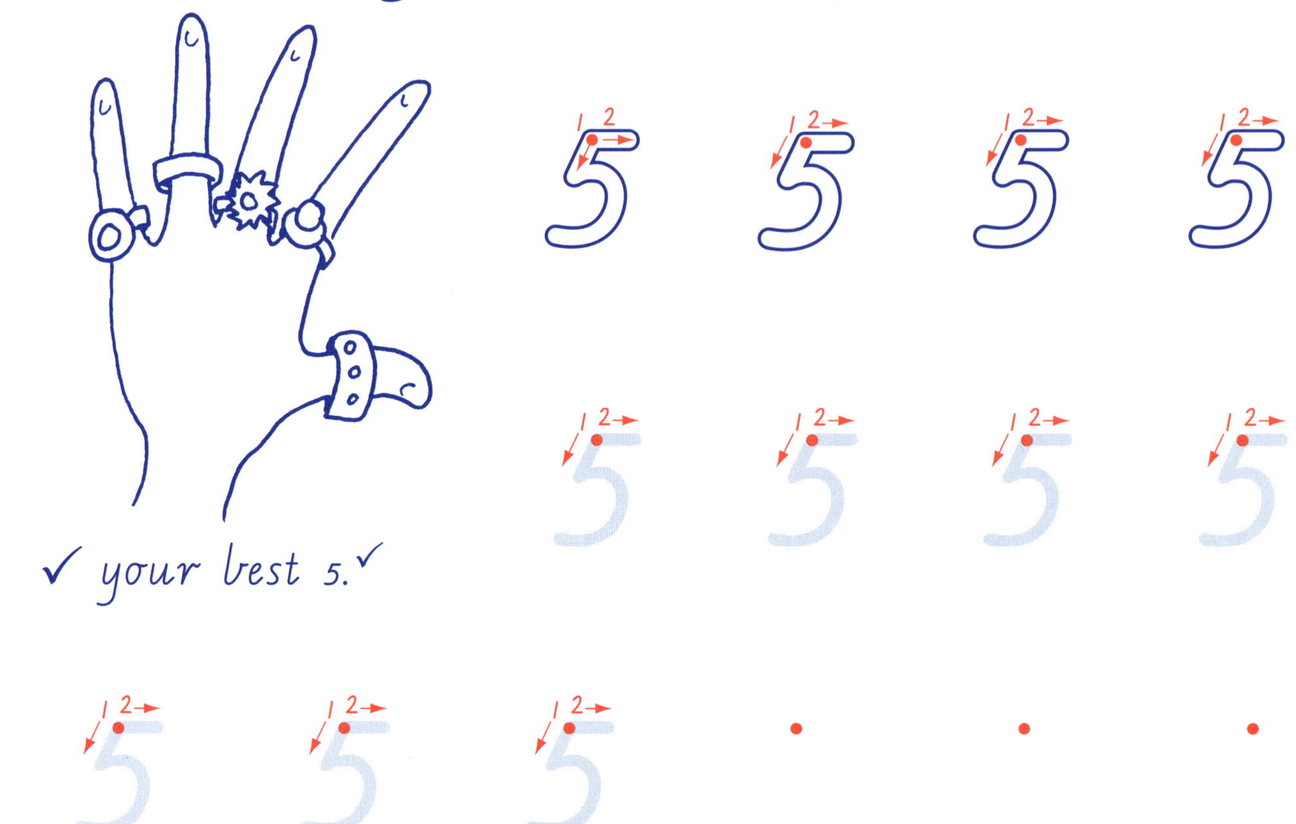

six legs on an insect

seven dwarfs

7 7 7 7 7 7

7 7 7

eight legs on an octopus

8 8 8

8 8 8

Circle your best 8.

8 8 8

nine wheels

✓ your best 9.✓

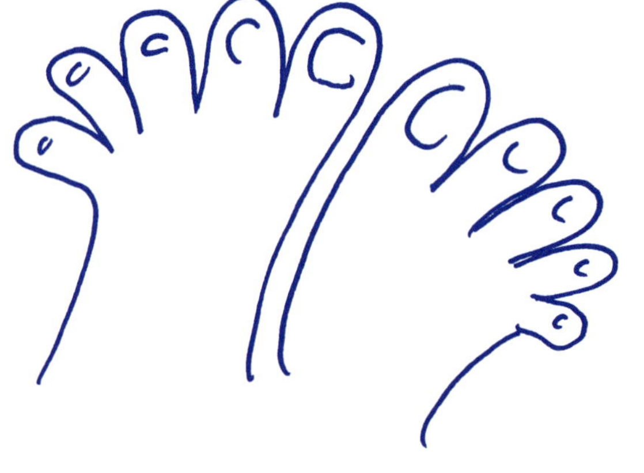

ten toes

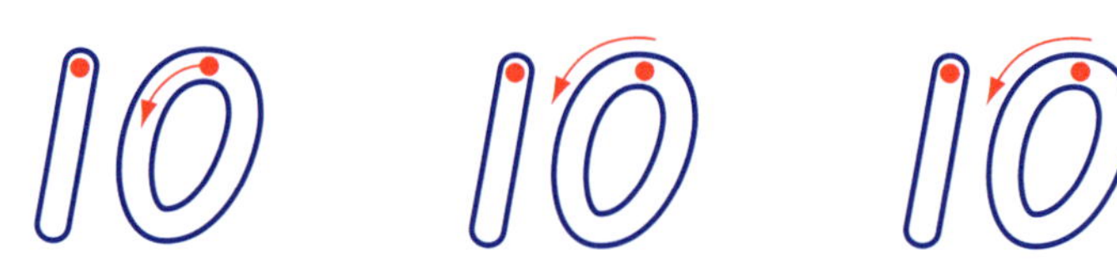